The Best of

Immor

"I ngersoll

Roger E Greeley

x/j

The Best of
Robert
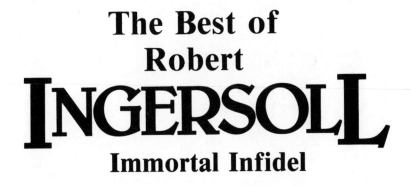
INGERSOLL
Immortal Infidel

Selections from his writings and speeches

edited by
Roger E. Greeley

Prometheus Books

700 East Amherst St. Buffalo, New York 14215

TO

Ed Wilson and all the others
who have kept freethought and
humanism alive.

Published 1983 by Prometheus Books
700 East Amherst Street, Buffalo, New York 14215

Library of Congress Catalog Number: 77-90495

ISBN: 0-87975-209-2

Printed in the United States of America

CONTENTS

My Creed

To love justice, to long for the right, to love mercy, to pity the suffering, to assist the weak, to forget wrongs and remember benefits—to love the truth, to be sincere, to utter honest words, to love liberty, to wage relentless war against slavery in all its forms, to love wife and child and friend, to make a happy home, to love the beautiful in art and in nature, to cultivate the mind, to be familiar with the mighty thoughts that genius has expressed and the noble deeds of all the world, to cultivate courage and cheerfulness, to make others happy, to fill life with the splendor of generous acts and the warmth of loving words, to discard error, to destroy prejudice, to receive new truths with gladness, to cultivate hope, to see the calm beyond the storm and the dawn beyond the night, to do the best that can be done and then to be resigned.

PREFACE

The year 1983 marks the sesquicentennial of the birth of America's premier orator and pioneer humanist, Robert Green Ingersoll. A century ago, Ingersoll was the most popular orator in the land. His lecture tours crisscrossed America, and each night he was greeted by audiences in which attendance was standing-room-only. In the nineteenth century no other orator spoke to so many so often as did the Great Agnostic.

Following his death in 1899 his speeches and interviews were collected in a twelve volume set. The years that followed witnessed more than seven editions of "The Complete Works of Robert Ingersoll" and seven biographies emerge from the press. Inspite of these efforts, the Great Agnostic is not well known in contemporary society. This is indeed unfortunate, because his active and fertile mind has much to offer us.

Ingersoll answered the Moral Majority over a century ago: intensely moral himself, he mercilessly attacked and exposed clerical hypocrisy and ignorance, the cruelties of Calvinism, and biblical absurdities. He sought to substitute the superiority of science and technology for the superstition and blind faith permeating his society. The clergy, unable to refute his arguments, resorted to calumny and epithets. Ironically, Ingersoll's popularity, fame, and fortune increased!

Just as Charles Darwin's work had questioned the assumptions of traditional science, Ingersoll's speeches struck the core of orthodox religion. In his iconoclastic attacks he performed a witty autopsy on the corpse of Calvinism, a theology lacking in relevant substance, with an inconsistent if not contradictory program of action. Though not himself a systematic, formal philosopher, Ingersoll's insights and acerbic wit advanced the cause of freethought thereby breaking the stranglehold superstition had placed upon thousands of victims of Calvin's suffocating and frightening theology.

As a political publicist Ingersoll had few peers and no superiors. Again and again he helped to ensure the election of Republicans to the White House. For years Ingersoll's political oratory was the standard by which all others were judged. His "Plumed Knight" speech, nominating James G. Blaine for the presidency, is an example of political rhetoric at its peak.

Possessing a commanding appearance, a magnificent speaking voice, and a keen wit, Ingersoll held audiences spellbound and speechless wherever and whenever he spoke. While attacking entrenched orthodoxy, he laid the foundation for the religion of the future, the religion of humanity. Humanism has not yet arrived; this fact would have surprised and disappointed Ingersoll.

Robert Green Ingersoll—soldier, lawyer, orator, humanitarian, and humanist—how we could use you today to counter the fundamentalist fanatics who continue to peddle the worst of Calvinist thought with all of its attendant miseries.

As you read Ingersoll you will laugh. More than that, you will shake your head in astonishment at his prescience and his thoroughly contemporary views on the rights of women, children, and minorities. His insights will give you live ammunition for today's debates. His public utterances were fearless and utterly frank. He was not one to employ euphemisms to soften his sledgehammer blows against orthodoxy. Ingersoll remains a refreshing oasis in the present desert of neo-orthodoxy and anachronistic fundamentalism. . . . Read and enjoy!

ACKNOWLEDGMENTS

There are several people whom I would like to thank for their assistance to me in preparing this book. Neil Gerdes, Librarian at Meadville/Lombard Theological School, literally opened the stacks to me. He also provided me with a letter of introduction that was a valuable key to other resources.

Dr. Gordon Stein, author of "The Ingersoll Checklist" has been a good friend and supporter throughout the final stages of this book.

In Peoria, the public library's Ingersoll collection is small but in excellent condition and readily accessible. The staff was most cooperative. The Peoria Historical Society was my next stop; and there, Connie Nagel spread a large feast of Ingersollia on very short notice.

In Springfield, at the Illinois State Historical Library, there is a gold mine of materials, and again the staff was most cooperative and patient. While researching in Springfield, I was the guest of the E. Raymond Stanhopes of nearby Decatur. An attorney and Ingersoll aficionado, he keeps Volume 12 of the *Complete Works of Robert Ingersoll* at his bedside! The researching in Springfield was thus made doubly rewarding by renewing an old friendship with the Stanhopeses.

Dr. David Curl, longtime friend and excellent photographer, is responsible for most of the pictures in this volume.

He worked hours refurbishing faded and ancient photographs. We drove down to Dowagiac where he took pictures of pictures too valuable to leave the library there. Also in Dowagiac, David Bainbridge, who tried to generate support for a museum to house the Beckwith Medallions, gave me a copy of the best picture of the historic Beckwith known to exist. He has spent hundreds of hours in pursuit of Beckwith's past. He, along with numberless townsfolk, shared their recollections of the incomparable theater with me. The senior citizens that I interviewed in two nursing homes in the area showed that, while specifics may fade with the years, one's general enthusiasm for the edifice remains alive forever.

When ex-Senator Hudson Sours of Peoria received me, he appeared to be in excellent health. A month later he suffered a fatal heart attack. I had been introduced to Senator Sours by Connie Nagel of the Peoria Historical Society. Senator Sours was the proud owner of an Ingersoll desk. We talked at some length about the Great Agnostic, and I asked the senator whether he thought a 150th anniversary celebration of Ingersoll's birth (August 11, 1833) might be appropriate at the site of the statue in Peoria's Glen Oak Park.

At best, life is uncertain. If there is a celebration in Peoria on August 11, 1983, let us hope that not only will Ingersoll be remembered, but that all those who loved him will be honored. Indeed, our greatest immortality lies in the lives of those who loved us.

INTRODUCTORY BIOGRAPHY

"Intellectual Freedom is Only the Right to Be Honest!"
Robert Green Ingersoll 1833-1899

On the afternoon of January 11, 1896, Col. Robert Green Ingersoll was treated to a guided tour of People's Church, Kalamazoo, Michigan. His guide was People's pastor, Caroline Bartlett (Crane). The church building was just a year old, and as a community center it impressed Ingersoll deeply. During a public lecture that night, the Great Agnostic departed from his scheduled remarks to make this observation concerning People's Church:

> It is the grandest thing in your state, if not in the United States. If there were a similar church near my home, I would join it, if its members would permit me.

This remark by Ingersoll prompted songs of exaltation in some of the most fundamentalist groups who had long been praying for his conversion. "Ingersoll converted," was the cry. Numerous inquiries arrived at Pastor Bartlett's study. Patiently, she tried to set the record straight. The wire services carried her explanation. The fundamentalists grew silent, even sullen. There was, after all, no "conversion to the true faith." People's Church was a creedless Unitarian church. Ingersoll had not been "saved" but he had discovered a simple institution whose aim was to be useful and helpful to people here and now. Later, when he was asked about his apparent endorsement of People's Church, Ingersoll reiterated his view:

> I visited the People's Church in Kalamazoo, Michigan. This church has no creed. The object is to make people happy in this world. Miss Bartlett is the pastor. She is a remarkable woman and is devoting her life to a good work. I liked her church and said so . . .

On September 15, 1957, I was ordained and installed as the minister of People's Church, Kalamazoo, Michigan. The creedless church which Ingersoll had applauded was still alive, creedless, and now was clearly humanistic. Where Ingersoll once stood, I took my religious oath of office.

I first became acquainted with the life and legacy of Robert Ingersoll while attending the General College of Boston University in 1946. Studying under the G.I. Bill, I had not yet decided on my life's work; it was to be either teaching or the ministry. As things developed, it was to be both! But never in those years of study did I ever dream that one day I would be the minister of People's Church.

Shortly after my ordination at People's in September of 1957, I ran across an account of Ingersoll's visit. Immediately, my interest in the man was rekindled. A local bookstore accepted my order for a "used set of Ingersoll's complete works in twelve volumes." Within the month I was the proud owner of a used but well-preserved set. What a gold mine for a Unitarian minister in his first year in the pulpit. I noticed that my set had markings indicating that it had once belonged to a small public library. I asked myself, "Why would a library dispose of such a good set?" After glancing through several volumes, the answer leapt from the pages. To many, Ingersoll remains a figure of extreme controversy, an infidel, an anti-Christ. Libraries that have the courage to retain his works often consign them to basement storage. His works remain inflammatory tracts to the fundamentalists. If he is this suspect in some circles today, what must his reception have been while he was alive and speaking!

Some suggest that Ingersoll is no longer controversial and

that the battle he fought was concluded even before the Scopes Trial in 1925. A careful and thorough reading of Ingersoll reveals that he remains a controversial, iconoclastic gadfly whose penetrating insights and keen commentaries are entirely relevant and appropriate to many of the emotionally charged issues of our time. An indefatigable speaker possessed of a photographic memory and a keen wit, brilliant trial lawyer, irrepressible infidel, and public lecturer without equal, Ingersoll commented on almost every significant issue of our nation between the elections of Lincoln and McKinley. Hence, the necessity for a twelve volume collection. Volume 10, for example, is devoted entirely to his most outstanding legal forensics. To suggest that one small volume could contain all of his trial oratory is absurd. The selections included present only his most outstanding cases.

Ingersoll did not, as is often maintained, restrict his commentaries to attacks upon the malevolent aspects of orthodox religion. Not at all. His observations on women and their rights, children, public education, science, the arts, crime and punishment, capital and labor, socialism, civil rights, civil liberties, marriage, and family reveal a breadth of interest and understanding that remains as fresh today as when he spoke in the nineteenth century.

Why is Robert Ingersoll not very well-known today? Often high school and college graduates alike, emerge from the rigors of academia never even having heard the name of one who spoke to more people than any other person in the last century. That fact alone would seem to dictate Ingersoll's inclusion in the annals of our nation; but more often than not he is not mentioned in classroom textbooks. His works are not often found in the circulating stacks of public libraries. Is it purely the law of supply and demand? I think not. Ingersoll created an enormous furor within orthodoxy as he systematically dissected and ridiculed the absurdities and fallacies of the Bible. Is this why he is largely unknown today? The common explanation as to why Ingersoll "died out" is that all of the evils he attacked in orthodoxy have been removed. The second and equally popular explanation for his being forgotten is his "intolerance." Many critics insist that his anti-clericalism exceeded the bounds of good taste, that—in fact—he was a bigot. In my judgment, neither explanation is particularly helpful or accurate. It is true that Ingersoll neither asked nor gave quarter in his disputations with men of the cloth. However, unlike his opponents, who showered him with vituperation and epithets, Ingersoll reserved his most penetrating sarcasm for ideas, institutions, and superstitions. He always had sympathy for the "victims" of orthodoxy but no sympathy whatsoever for orthodoxy itself. He was always careful to distinguish between belief and believer. He pitied those he regarded as "the prisoners of a cruel God."

At present to question the sincere beliefs of others is considered to be intolerant. Today, the free market of ideas and their vigorous debate stops on the threshold of the church. Religion and theology are truly off-limits, protected by an artificial sanctuary of "tolerance" and what is considered to be "mutual respect." Ingersoll would have contested this special treatment extended to "religious truth." His opinion was that until we were emancipated from all superstition and falsehoods, the human race would not, could not, accept full responsibility for its destiny on planet earth. To this end, Ingersoll maintained that no area of human thought was to be free from ruthless and honest inquiry and equally open debate.

Have things actually changed in the church-world as much as some would have us believe? How would Ingersoll respond to Billy Graham, Oral Roberts or Rex Humbard? Does not this trinity reach more people, and enjoy more support, than any Bible-thumpers in our history? Could Ingersoll obtain equal time on TV? Who would pay the bills? How would he respond to those demanding the inclusion of the Creationist theory in all public school biology classes? Speaking of public education, on which side would Ingersoll be in the long battle surrounding prayers in the classroom? What of Parochiaid? What about a woman's right to abortion on demand? Surely, he would have championed the crusade of the oft-imprisoned Margaret Sanger. He, in fact, predicted the scientific breakthrough that would make "woman the mistress of her own body." Would Ingersoll have been one to applaud the modification of our pledge of allegiance to include the words, "under God"? Would he view the continuance of tax exemption for churches as a victory for the absolute separation of church and state? Obviously, from this very sketchy list of recent concerns, Ingersoll did not fade from view because radical reform had spiked his guns. No, we will have to look still further to account for his having been largely forgotten and overlooked by historians and authors of textbooks in American history.

Some maintain that Ingersoll's message was inseparable from his magnificent voice and that when he died and the great voice was forever stilled, the message it carried accompanied him to the crematorium. That his was a magnificent voice not even his severest critics denied. The tributes and accolades given on the occasion of his death (and on many other occasions before he died) by scores of distinguished citizens are ample testimony to the glory of his magnificent voice. It is said that simply to read his speeches is to miss much of what was incorporated in their delivery. Undoubtedly, there is substantial truth in this assertion. The error in this analysis is that it completely overlooks the *substance* of what Ingersoll said. For eighteen years, I have been turning to the twelve volumes for his insights and commentaries, wit and wisdom. Rarely, have I come away empty-handed. Nearly always there is an entry bearing directly on some pressing concern of today. As an absolute believer in free speech he set standards that we have yet to achieve. It is most unlikely that he would have supported the Smith Act, not because he was sympathetic to Communism—he was not—but because he was a Jeffersonian in matters of free speech. The belief that Ingersoll was forgotten because of the inseparability of the message from its execution is not valid. We must look to yet other reasons for why Ingersoll is largely unknown in America today.

The day following his death, the prestigious *New York Times* devoted a long editorial to his controversial career, which had ended suddenly and unexpectedly while summering at Dobbs Ferry, New York. The spirit of the editorial is expressed completely in the final paragraph:

> The lack of respect in which he exalted was his bane, that by reason of it and of his free exhibition of it he never took the place in the social, the professional, or the public life of his

country to which, by his talents he otherwise would have been eminently entitled. (*New York Times* July 22, 1899)

Certainly the *Times*'s editorial spoke for the establishment in and out of religion. The accolades and loving tributes came from dissidents, nonconformists, activists, radicals, free thinkers, individualists and reformers. Consider the lives and individualism of the following people, each of whom respected Ingersoll and deeply mourned his sudden death: Susan B. Anthony, Luther Burbank, Carrie Chapman Catt, Eugene Debs, Clarence Darrow, Thomas Edison, Hamlin Garland, George Holyoake, Edwin Markham, Edgar Lee Masters, Margaret Sanger, Elizabeth Cady Stanton, and Mark Twain. This list is far from complete, but its members have survived the test of time. Independent, creative free spirits, they knew that they had lost a friend, a leader in the cause of enlightened humanitarianism. Certainly, had he been alive, Walt Whitman would have sent his condolences, for he greatly admired Ingersoll. When Whitman died in 1892, Ingersoll was in Canada on a lecture tour. He travelled day and night, arriving at Camden, New Jersey, in time to give a beautiful eulogy, closing with the observation: "Long-after we are dead the brave words he has spoken will sound like trumpets to the dying. And so I lay this little wreath upon this great man's tomb. I loved him living, and I love him still."

Hundreds, no thousands, of letters and cables came to Ingersoll's grieving widow Eva and her two daughters Maud and Eva. How many of these simple tributes and expressions of deep affection were from citizens who had never met the Colonel? "Dear Mrs. Ingersoll, you don't know me but I once heard your dear husband speak in our town. His words changed my life and I just wanted you to know how much I shall always treasure his memory. He was a great and kind man." If you multiply this sentiment by several thousand, you have a partial picture of what influence Ingersoll exerted on the lives of thousands who had been walking around bent over by superstition's yoke. How many he liberated! How many he freed! The common people knew their champion and loved him.

The general reaction of the "establishment press" reflected the bigotry of the conforming majority. The majority has al-

ways found it difficult to accept individualists, debunkers, icon-
oclasts, innovators, dissidents and reformers, regardless of the
merit of their causes. The cruelties visited upon the suffragists,
the early organizers of labor, and above all others the courageous Margaret Sanger are the trademark of conforming con-
servatism throughout our history. Remember, the incomparable Margaret Sanger was jailed many times for merely
seeking to extend the right to birth control information to all
who sought it. Superstition stands ready to open the prison's
door to those who dare to challenge her. Remember, too, that
while Theodore Roosevelt was villifying the memory of Thomas
Paine, calling him that "filthy little atheist," Ingersoll was
eulogizing the author of "Common Sense." Ingersoll's confidence in the ultimate acceptance by this nation of Paine's
proper place was vindicated in 1945 when, at last, Paine entered
the Hall of Fame of Great Americans, 136 years after his death!
We might well ask, will it be the year 2035 (or later) before we
formally acknowledge the greatness and humanitarianism of
Robert Green Ingersoll? (Two resolutions to this end died in
Congress in the early 1930s.)

Ingersoll made the majority uncomfortable. The majority
preferred to misunderstand him, for to understand him would
require a substantial revision and repudiation of many comfort-
ing illusions, lovely lies, and supportive superstitions. Most
people preferred to accept old traditions with an embarrassed
silence rather than join with the Great Agnostic. After all, what
if Ingersoll was wrong and orthodoxy was right? Surely, there
would be hell to pay! It took strength of character then (and it
still does) to challenge and question the validity and value of the
moss-covered idols of the tribe. There was yet another aspect of
the gospel of the "infidel" for which many never could forgive
him, whether he was right or not: his utter rejection of a future
life in heaven or hell. Personally, he cherished the idea of immortality. He did not, however, allow his personal wishes and
hopes to become the "facts" of his religion of humanity; nor
were his hopes palmed off as facts under the pressure of delivering a eulogy for dear friends or relatives. Thus, though he never
did deny the eternal hope for immortaility that lies within the
human breast, his refusal to posit an eternal life along biblical

lines was seized upon by many as proof of his wholesale rejection of all religion. This was (and is) as unjust as it was inaccurate and simplistic. Ingersoll was, by the concepts of contemporary religious humanism, an intensely religious man. Only those who refuse to accept humanism as a religion find Ingersoll "irreligious." In view of this, one may well ask Who is and who is not "tolerant"?

Millions cannot accept a basic tenet of contemporary religious humanism: immortality as continuing personal existence beyond the grave is an unproved and unprovable theological myth. Many human beings need and demand more than a life that ends at the grave. Ingersoll himself entertained the hope of immortality to the very last. Yet, standing higher than this hope was the absolute integrity of his reason. He could not and did not compromise his intellectual integrity to accommodate his emotional needs. This demands enormous strength of character. It requires a sacrifice that few have been willing to make. Regretfully but realistically, Ingersoll accepted the reality of human grief and suggested gentler and more loving lives as the only rational alternative to positing paradisiacal palaces or hell's holy holocaust in the hereafter. It was this very uneasiness he created that was to deprive his legacy of extended longevity. It also created ambivalent feelings among timid intellectuals who could not quite bring themselves to his free thought. Writing in 1909, Michael Monahan put it very well:

> The circle of the man's philanthropy was complete. He filled the measure of patriotism, of civic duty, of the sacred relations of husband and father, of generosity and kindness toward his fellowman. But he committed treason against the Unknown, and this, in spite of the fame and success which his talents commanded, made of him a social Pariah. The herd admired and envied his freedom, but for the most part, they gave him the road and went by on the other side.

Yes, Mr. Monahan seems to have put his finger on the very heart of the matter. Today, as then, millions prefer blind promises to honest expressions (and admissions) of the limits of human knowledge about life after death. In the years since he died, nothing has changed regarding the facts to refute Ingersoll's agnosticism concerning personal immortality. Were he alive and speaking today, he would find it just as difficult to win converts to his religion of humanity, a religion that begins in the cradle and ends at the grave. Life does not become eternal simply because we wish it to be. That the wish is eternal no one will deny. Ingersoll insisted that eternity had no bearing on virtuous living here and now; immortality was not the prize for a loving life; if it existed at all, it was a fact of nature, not of creed. That life is eternal has not been established with evidence derived from the natural universe. Thus we have not advanced a millimeter since Ingersoll breathed his last.

There were yet other aspects of Ingersoll which irritated his contemporaries. He made "good people" very uncomfortable about their white racism. He was absolutely uncompromising on the hypocrisy and immorality of the institution of slavery, which had biblical endorsement. When slavery was abolished by constitutional amendment, he was not satisfied. He then attacked with equal vigor *all* forms of Jim Crowism and second-class citizenship. He accepted literally and without reservation the promises contained in the Declaration of Independence and the Gettysburg Address. He was at home with all colors and minorities and with both sexes. In the nineteenth century women had no greater champion among men than Ingersoll. Though he generally used the word "men" in his speeches, one need only read his commentaries on women to appreciate his total commitment to their quest for equal rights and first-class citizenship. If anything, he was slightly prejudiced against men!

There is yet another dimension to this incredible man that earned him the enmity of many an establishment figure in charge of the organs of communication. In the Gilded Age, to be an unqualified sympathizer to the laboring person was hardly a calling card to the society of the robber barons. Ingersoll, however, did not embrace any "ism" as the working man's passport to a civilized lifestyle. He rejected all these, for their dogmatism reminded him of orthodox religion. He found them to be too simplistic, naive and radically destructive. Depending upon the convictions of the listener, he was classified as a hopeless conservative or a radical revolutionary. He was neither; he was by self-definition simply an individualist. His confidence in reason, education, science, and the ballot led him to the conclusion that neither "isms" nor charity were panaceas. Perfecting the democratic process was the surest way out for the oppressed, whatever their endeavor, wherever their livelihood. While he and Eugene Debs enjoyed the highest regard and affection for one another, they were worlds apart in their separate means to a common end: the improvement of the human condition on earth, here and now.

Certainly Ingersoll would have been better remembered had he stayed with politics, a career that some believed would lead him to the White House itself. Again, his agnosticism precluded and cut short his role as a politician. He became a celebrated publicist for the candidacies of others. His famous "Plumed Knight" speech nominating James Blaine for president was the standard by which convention rhetoric was judged for two decades. He turned to promoting others when it was clear that he would have to renounce his religious agnosticism if he were to gain favor with the professional politicians. He could not do it. If he had to choose between running for office and maintaining the integrity of his own mind, there was no choice to be made. In this light, we might now ask what our vaunted freedom of religion actually means when its exercise in the market place has this crippling effect upon political aspirations. Historians are quick to point out that it is doubtful that a religious nonconformist such as Thomas Jefferson (Unitarian) could obtain, today, nomination without a more respectable church affiliation. (Do you recall the religious odyssey of one Adlai Stevenson in his two tries for the presidency?) While a military man, Dwight Eisenhower had felt no compelling need to be a church member; but when the White House beckoned, he quickly embraced an organized church. Is there not something to be regretted in religious conviction as a ticket to political stardom? The "straw men" Ingersoll was accused of attacking in his time would appear to be very much alive today.

Ingersoll has been criticized frequently because he was simply "against orthodox religion." Had this been the sum total of his labors, the criticism would have some merit, though not much. Anyone who has read his works will see at once the absurdity of such a criticism. Ingersoll was a champion of what he called the religion of humanity, better known as humanism today. When the *New York Times* stated in its editorial that he "lacked respect," he would have been the first to admit that he did not respect superstition, slavery, the supernatural, ignorance, cruelty, stupidity, caste, class, polygamy, revenge, punishment, eternal damnation, Calvinist predestination, injustice, poverty, want and suffering, disease and benevolent design in the universe. While admitting that he did not "respect" these, he clearly was truly reverent in his regard for science, human liberty, the natural universe, equitable distribution of profits and Nature's storehouse, love family, fellowship, the arts, kindness, justice, monogamy, the rights of women and children, reason, knowledge, education, investigation, sobriety, labor, and usefulness. He did not respect, in fact he hated, hypocrisy and all it carried on its back.

He did not work out a detailed and systematic philosophical system for his religion of humanity. Ingersoll was not a professional philosopher. He was an activist, a provoker, a prodder, an exhorter, a champion of causes and underdogs, a crusader for the absolute enfranchisement of human reason. He had no "respect" for blind faith and even less "respect" for obedience to the dictates of blind faith. Yet, in his own moral conduct, his own character adhered to the most demanding standards of the most orthodox faith (with the possible exception of his love of billiards, cigars, and the theater). When he declared again and again that "intelligence is the only lever that can raise mankind," he meant to contest any and all things that crippled the exercise of reason in all theaters of human endeavor, beginning with organized religion. He wanted the church to be honest and to think for today in today's world, with today's knowledge of that world. He could not respect ignorance because it had enjoyed longevity. He worshipped, instead, the quest for the truth, the growth of human knowledge, and the spread of science. He had no confidence in orthodox churches, charities, or "isms." He saw mankind's future as entirely dependent on the exercise of reason welded to science and diffused through universal free public education. His attitude towards government was essentially Jeffersonian, that is, that government exists to protect one from injury from one's neighbor. The abuses of the industrial revolution of the Gilded Age altered his views of the role of government, and it would have been delightful to see how he would have reacted to Teddy Roosevelt's trust-busting and other reforms of the muckraking era.

Ingersoll was an agnostic and not an atheist. Although this distinction was lost on him, his utterances clearly mark him as one who maintains that, "God is unknown and unknowable," rather than one who declares absolutely, "There is no God." The "true believers," however, see no distinction between the two positions and ostracize both with equal scorn and disapproval. Unless your own religious orientation is very narrow, rigid, and traditional, you will probably view Ingersoll as a deeply religious man before you have finished this book. If religion consists of living an honest, useful, and loving life and seeking to add to our knowledge of ourselves and planet earth, then Robert Ingersoll was a deeply religious man. If, instead, it is believed that religion is the guarantee of a next-life for those who have memorized the proper passwords, Ingersoll is not, by these narrow standards, "religious." Ingersoll is for those who thrill to the legacy of liberating the mind and body of every human being. He is for those who find inspiration in the lives of all who have tried to shed light on the human predicament, who have inched humanity forward by their loving labors.

In this book, I have tried to include, from the complete works, letters, other papers, and newspaper articles, quotations that are pertinent for their contemporary applicability, that are delightful for their wit and gifted language, and finally, are representative of Ingersoll's absolute intellectual integrity and his commitment to the religion of humanity.

We have a long way to go before we catch up to Ingersoll's vision of a truly liberated people. Though he died in 1899, many of his commentaries remain ahead of us, yet to be fulfilled. Indeed he was a prophet, a man of courage, and a loving humanitarian.

Lastly, do not attempt to put Ingersoll into the pigeonhole of any party, position, "ism," or platform. It will not work. He will surprise you every time with what appears to be a contradiction. It is not. As is written on the title page of Volume 8:

> This is my creed:
> Happiness is the only good; reason the only torch, justice the only worship, humanity the only religion, and love the only priest.

Under this philosophical umbrella, the whole of Ingersoll is to be discovered and enjoyed, simply this and nothing more. Enjoy!

CHAPTER ONE

QUOTATIONS FROM ROBERT INGERSOLL, ARRANGED ALPHABETICALLY BY SUBJECT

Introduction: About the Quotations

Unless otherwise indicated, the quotations presented in this book are taken from *The Complete Works of Robert Ingersoll,* in twelve volumes, The First Dresden Edition, published in 1900.

In an attempt to make the text as readable as possible, specific page and volume references have been omitted. In piecing together quotes, while no substantive material has been altered, arrangement has followed the desire to compress and include as many as possible in the available space. Sometimes I have inserted the name of the subject to which Ingersoll was making reference while in an extended paragraph he may have referred to it specifically only once and the balance of the time as "it" or "they."

Lastly, I must regretfully acknowledge that very possibly some of the best examples of Ingersoll's phrasing and expression may not be in this volume; some of my own favorites are not here, but one has to draw the line someplace. Perhaps you will be prompted to acquire the twelve volumes and make your own additions! I do not think you will discover any significant omission of subject matter. I have endeavored to cover the wit and wisdom of Ingersoll that is entirely relevant to our time.

Adam and Eve

Unless the Lord God was looking for a helpmeet for Adam, why did he cause the animals to pass before him. And why did he, after the menagerie had passed by, pathetically exclaim, "But for Adam there was not found a helpmeet for him"? It seems that Adam saw nothing that struck his fancy. The fairest ape, the sprightliest chimpanzee, the loveliest baboon, the most bewitching orangoutang, the most fascinating gorilla failed to touch with love's sweet pain, poor Adam's lonely heart. Let us rejoice that this was so. Had he fallen in love then, there never would have been a Freethinker in the world . . . .

Imagine the Lord God with a bone in his hand with which to start a woman, trying to make up his mind whether to make a blond or a brunette! . . . These stories must be believed, or the work of regeneration can never be commenced.

Agnostic(s)

The Agnostic . . . occupies himself with this world, with things that can be ascertained and understood. He turns his attention to the sciences, to the solutions of questions that touch the well-being of man. He wishes to prevent and cure disease; to lengthen life; to provide homes and raiment and food for man; to supply the wants of the body. He also cultivates the arts. He believes in painting and sculpture, in music and the drama—the needs of the soul. The Agnostic believes in developing the brain, in cultivating the affections, the tastes, the conscience, the judgement, to the end that man may be happy in this world.

Unless it can be shown that atheism interferes with sight, hearing, or memory, why should justice shut the door to truth?

In most of the states of this union, I could not give testimony. Christianity has such a contemptable opinion of human nature that it does not believe that a man can tell the truth unless frightened by a belief in God. [Response to fact that declared atheists cannot give testimony in legal proceedings.] After all the Agnostic and the Positivist have the same end in view—both believe in living for this world.

The Agnostic does not simply say, "I do not know." He goes another step and says with great emphasis that you do not know.

Alcoholism

I believe that by the long and continuous use of stimulants, the system gets in such a condition that it imperatively demands not only the usual, but an increased stimulant. After a time, every nerve becomes hungry, and there is in the body of the man a cry, coming from every nerve for nourishment. There is a kind of famine and unless the want is supplied, insanity is the result. This hunger of the nerves drowns the voice of reason—cares nothing for argument—nothing for experience—nothing for the sufferings of others—nothing for anything, except for the food it requires. Words are wasted; advice is of no possible use; argument is like reasoning with the dead. The man has lost control of his will—it has been won over to the side of the nerves. He imagines that if the nerves are once satisfied he can then resume control of himself. Of course, this is a mistake, and the more the nerves are satisfied the more imperative is their demand. Arguments are not of the slightest force. The knowledge—the conviction—the course pursued is wrong has no effect. So the fact that the man knows that he should not drink has not the slightest effect upon him. The sophistry of passion outweighs all that reason can urge. In other words, the man is the victim of disease until the disease is arrested, his will is not his own. He may wish to reform but wish is not will. I believe that science is to become the basis, and if only we knew enough of the human system—of the tides and currents of thought and will and wish—enough of the storms of passion—if we only knew how the brain acts and operates—if we only knew the relation between blood and thought, between thought and act—if we only knew the conditions of conduct, then we could, through science, control the passions of the human race.

Arts (The)

I have always loved the theater—loved the stage simply because it has added to the happiness of life . . . the theater is a splendid, great instrumentality for increasing the well-being of man.

The stage has ever been the altar, the pulpit, the cathedral of the heart.

The drama is the crystallization of history, an epitome of the human heart. The past is lived again and again, and we see upon the stage, love, sacrifice, fidelity, courage—all the virtues mingled with the follies . . . what is the great thing that the stage does? It cultivates the imagination . . . imagination is the mother of pity, the mother of generosity, the mother of every possible virtue. It is by the imagination that you are able to put yourself in the place of another.

Nearly all the arts unite in theater, and it is the result of the best, the highest, the most artistic, that man can do.

Imagination is the mother of enthusiasm. Imagination fans the little spark into a flame great enough to warm the human race; and enthusiasm is to the mind what spring is to the world.

I enjoy the stage; I always did enjoy it. I love the humanity of it. I hate solemnity; it is the brother of stupidity—always. Only a few years ago our ancestors looked upon the theater as the vestibule of hell.

Wagner is the Shakespeare of music. The funeral music for Siegfried is the funeral music for all the dead. Should all the gods die, this music would be perfectly appropriate. It is elemental, universal, eternal. Wagner was a sculptor, a painter in sound.

I regard opera as one of the great civilizers. No one can listen to the symphonies of Beethoven, or the music of Schubert, without receiving a benefit. And no one can hear the operas of Wagner without feeling he has been ennobled and refined.

Art has nothing to do directly with morality or immorality. It is its own excuse for being, it exists for itself. Art accomplishes by indirection; the beautiful refines.

All art, in my judgement, is for the sake of expression.

The marbles of Greece have not been equalled. They still occupy niches dedicated to perfection.

The office of Poet Laureate (in England) should be abolished. Men cannot write poems to order as they could deliver cabbages or beer. By poems I do not mean jangles of words. I mean great thoughts clothed in splendor.

The object of the artist is to present truthfully and artistically. He is not a Sunday School teacher. He is not to have moral effect eternally in his mind. It is enough for him to be truly artistic. Because, as I have said, a great many times, the greatest good is done by indirection.

Authorship of the New Testament

Christ never wrote a solitary word of the New Testament—not one word. There is an account that he once stooped and wrote something in the sand, but that has not been preserved. He never told anybody to write a word. He never said, "Matthew, remember this. Mark, do not forget to put that down. Luke, be sure in your gospel you have this. John, do not forget it." Not one word. And it has always seemed to me that a being coming from another world, with a message of infinite importance to mankind, should at least have verified that message by his own signature. Is it not wonderful that not one word was written by Christ? Is it not strange that he gave no orders to have his words preserved—words upon which hung the salvation of the world?

Why was it that the disciples of Christ wrote in Greek, whereas, in fact, they understood only Hebrew?

Bearing False Witness

Is it ever right to lie? Of course, sometimes. In war when a man is captured by the enemy he ought to lie to them to mislead them. What we call strategy is nothing more than lies. For the accomplishment of a good end, for instance, the saving of a woman's reputation, it is many times, perfectly right to lie. As a rule, people ought to tell the truth. If it is right to kill a man to save your own life it certainly ought to be right to fool him for the same purpose. I would rather be deceived than killed, wouldn't you?

Bible (The)

I do not throw away the Bible because there are some foolish passages in it, but I say, throw away the foolish passages. Don't throw away wisdom because it is found in the company of folly; but do not say that folly is wisdom because it is found in its company.

I know that religious people cling to the Bible on account of the good that is in it, and in spite of the bad. I know that Freethinkers throw away the Bible on account of the bad in it, in spite of the good. I hope the time will come when the book will be treated like other books and will be judged upon its merits, apart from the fiction of inspiration.

I admit that there are many good and beautiful passages in the Old and New Testaments; that from the lips of Christ dropped many pearls of kindness—of love. Every verse that is true and tender I treasure in my heart. Every thought, behind which is the tear of pity, I appreciate and love.

If a man would follow, today, the teachings of the Old Testament he would be a criminal. If he would strictly follow the teachings of the New, he would be insane.

The Bible is not inspired in its morality, for the reason that slavery is not moral, that polygamy is not good, that wars of extermination are not merciful, and that nothing can be more immoral than to punish the innocent on account of the sins of the guilty.

If the Bible is true, man is a special creation, and if man is a special creation, millions of facts must have conspired millions of ages ago, to deceive the scientific world of today.

Nothing in the inspired book is so dangerous as accuracy.

Suppose there were no passages in the Bible except those upholding slavery, polygamy, and wars of extermination, would anybody claim that it was the word of God? I would like to ask if there is a Christian in the world who would not be overjoyed to find that every one of these passages was an interpolation?

In a few years you will take the Bible for what it is worth. The good and the true will be treasured in the heart, the foolish, the infamous, will be thrown away.

Birth Control

Through the intelligent practice of birth control and voluntary parenthood, disease and crime may yet be prevented from conquering the world. Through emancipation of women, "ignorance, poverty, and vice" might "stop populating the world".

Blasphemy

What is blasphemy in one country would be a religious exhortation in another. Blasphemy is the word that the majority hisses into the ears of the few. Each church has accused nearly every other of being a blasphemer. The Catholics called Martin Luther a blasphemer and Martin Luther called Copernicus a blasphemer. Pious ignorance always regards intelligence as a kind of blasphemy. Some of the greatest men of the world, some of the best, have been put to death for blasphemy. After every argument of the church has been answered, has been refuted, then the church cries, "Blasphemy." Blasphemy is what an old mistake says of a newly discovered truth. Blasphemy is the bulwark of religious prejudice. Blasphemy is the breastplate of the heartless. The Infinite cannot be blasphemed.

Editor's Note: The occasion for these remarks on "blasphemy" was the trial of a young man charged with blasphemy under an ancient New Jersey statute. The trial took place in 1887. Ingersoll's summation lasted some four hours—in a losing cause. The jury, of course, found the defendant guilty and the judge imposed a fine of $25 and court costs of $75, all of which Ingersoll paid, giving his own services without charge!

The cry of blasphemy means only that the argument of the blasphemer cannot be answered. Blasphemy is what last year's leaf says to this year's bud.

Question directed to Ingersoll: "Col., is it true that you were once threatened with a criminal prosecution for libel on religion?" "Yes, in Delaware. Chief Justice Comegys instructed the grand jury to indict me for blasphemy. I have taken my revenge on that state by leaving it in ignorance."

Comments on Celebrated Persons

Miss Anthony (Susan B.) is one of the most remarkable women in the world. She has the enthusiasm of youth and spring, the courage and sincerity of a martyr. She is as reliable as the attraction of gravitation. She is absolutely true to her convictions, intellectually honest, logical, candid, and infinitely persistent. No human being has done more for women than Miss Anthony. She has won the respect and admiration of the best people of the earth. And so I say: "Good luck and long life to Susan B. Anthony."

There is not a Universalist who does not worship Hosea Ballou. I love him myself because he said to a Presbyterian minister: "You are going around trying to keep people out of hell, and I am going around trying to keep hell out of people." Every Universalist admires him and loves him because when despised and railed and spit upon, he stood firm a patient witness for the eternal mercy of God.

Henry Ward Beecher was born in a Puritan penitentiary, of which his father was one of the wardens . . . He was the greatest orator that stood within the pulpit's narrow curve. He loved liberty of speech. There was no trace of bigot in his blood. He was a brave and generous man. I regard him as the greatest man in any pulpit. He treated me with a generosity that nothing can exceed.

I suppose that Mr. Beecher is the greatest man in the pulpit. He thinks more of Darwin than he does of David and has an idea that the Old Testament is just a little too old. He has put evolution in the place of atonement—has thrown away the Garden of Eden, snake, apples, and all, and is endeavoring to save enough of the orthodox wreck to make a raft. I know of no other genius in the pulpit.

The glory of Jeremy Benthem is, that he gave the true basis of morals, and furnished statesmen with the star and compass of this sentence: "The greatest happiness of the greatest number."

Henry Bergh did as much good as any man who has lived in the 19th century. (cruelty to animals)

Mrs. Browning was far greater than her husband.

Robert Burns: We meet here tonight to honor the memory of a poet—possibly the next to the greatest that has ever written in our language. I would place one above him, and only one—Shakespeare.

Giordano Bruno, the greatest of martyrs, visited London in Shakespeare's time, delivered lectures at Oxford, and called the institution, "the widow of learning".

John Calvin was of a pallid, bloodless complexion, thin, sickly, irritable, gloomy, impatient, egotistic, tyrannical, heartless, and infamous. He was a strange compound of revengeful morality, malicious forgiveness, ferocious charity, egotistic humility, and a kind of hellish justice. In other words, he was as near like the God of the Old Testament as his health permitted.

Charlemagne had laws against polygamy yet practised it himself.

Had such men as Robert Collyer and John Stuart Mill been present at the burning of Servetus, they would have extinguished the flames with their tears.

It is easy to understand the splendid dream of August Comte. Is the human race worthy to be worshipped by itself—that is to say, should the individual worship himself? Certainly the religion of humanity is better than the religion of the inhuman . . . The mission of Positivism is, in the language of its founder, "To generalize science and systematize sociality" . . . The Agnostic and the Positivist have the same end in view—both believe in living for this world.

The laurel of the 19th century is on Darwin's brow.

In my judgement, Charles Dickens wrote the greatest novels.

Disraeli's books (novels) will—in a little while—follow their author into the grave. After all, the good will live longest.

T. H. Huxley wrote like a trained swordsman.

Abraham Lincoln was, in my judgement, in many respects the grandest man ever President of the United States . . . Upon his monument these words should be written: "Here sleeps the only man in the history of the world who, having almost absolute power, never abused it except on the side of mercy."

Thomas Paine was great. Thomas Paine was a hero. A few more years—a few brave men—a few more rays of light, and mankind will venerate the memory of him.

Editor's Note: This statement was made shortly before Teddy Roosevelt referred to Paine as "that filthy little atheist!" Thomas Paine was elected to the Hall of Fame of Great Americans in 1945.

I have great respect for the memory of Theodore Parker. Theodore Parker was a great orator. When he spoke of freedom, of duty, of living to the ideal, of mental integrity; he seemed inspired.

The Queen is clothed in garments given to her by blind fortune and unreasoning chance. George Eliot wears robes of glory, woven in the loom of her own genius.

[In a letter to Elizabeth Cady Stanton]: I am in favor of giving every right to women that I claim for myself, and I shall vote to do that if I ever have the chance. Rest assured, I am on your side and will vote your way and will give you aid and comfort—and let you do the speaking.

When Charles Sumner, that splendid publicist—Charles Sumner, the philanthropist, one who spoke of the conscience of his time and to the history of the future—when he stood up in the U.S. Senate and made a glorious plea for human liberty, there crept into the Senate a villain and struck him down as though he was a wild beast.

The trouble with Swedenborg was that he changed realities into dreams, and then out of his dream made facts upon which he built, and with which he constructed his system.

I enjoy Shakespeare everywhere. I think it would give me pleasure to hear those wonderful lines spoken even by the phonograph. There is more beauty, more goodness, more intelligence in Shakespeare than in all the sacred books of this world.

Voltaire was the greatest man of his century, and did more to free the human race than any other of the sons of men.

I do not believe that the music of Wagner will ever be excelled.

Daniel Webster worshipped the past. He kept his back to the sunrise. He was not true to his ideal. He talked sometimes as though his head was among the stars but he stood in the gutter . . . He defended the Fugitive Slave law.

Walt Whitman: He was built on a broad and splendid plan—ample, without appearing to have limitations—passing easily for a brother of the mountains and seas and constellations: caring nothing for the little maps and charts with which timid pilots hug the shore, but giving himself freely with recklessness of genius to winds and waves and tides, caring for nothing as long as the stars were above him. Walt Whitman utters the elemental truths and is the poet of democracy. He is also the poet of individuality.

No American should fail to honor Roger Williams. He was the first grand advocate of the liberty of the soul. He was in favor of the eternal divorce of church and state.

[Response to the Zola/Dreyfuss affair]: It was one of the most infamous trials in the history of the world. Zola is a great man, a genius, the best man in France. His trial was a travesty on justice. The judge acted like a bandit. The proceedings were a disgrace to human nature. The jurors must have been ignorant beasts. The French have disgraced themselves. Long live Zola.

Editor's Note: Just five days after Ingersoll died, Dreyfuss was declared innocent.

Children

I tell you children have the same rights that we have, and we ought to treat them as though they were human beings. They should be reared with love and kindness, with tenderness, and not with brutality.

Do not treat your children like orthodox posts to be set in a row. Treat them like trees that need light and sun and air. Be fair and honest with them; give them a chance. Recollect that their rights are equal to yours. Do not have it in your mind that you must govern them; that they must obey. Throw away forever the idea of master and slave.

We must educate the children, rescue them from ignorance and crime. Schoolhouses are the real temples and teachers are the true priests. Let us develop the brain, civilize the heart, and give wings to the imagination.

Teach your children the facts that you know. If you do not know, say so. Be as honest as you are ignorant. Do all you can to develop their minds to the end that they may live useful, happy lives. Teach them the world is natural. Teach them to be absolutely honest. Do not send them where they will contract diseases of the mind—the leprosy of the soul. Let us do all we can to make them intelligent.

The whip degrades; a severe father teaches his children to dissemble; their love is pretense, and their obedience a species of self-defense. Fear is the father of lies.

All children should be the children of love. All that are born should be sincerely welcomed.

Christ

If Christ, in fact, said, "I came not to bring peace but a sword," it is the only prophecy in the New Testament that has been literally fulfilled.

Christ takes his appropriate place with the other teachers of mankind. His life becomes reasonable and admirable. We have a man who hated oppression; who despised and denounced superstition and hypocrisy; who attacked the heartless church of his time; who excited the hatred of bigots and priests, and who rather than be false to his conception of truth, met and even bravely suffered even death.

In his day, Christ was an Infidel, and made himself unpopular by denouncing the church as it then existed. Christ will never again visit the earth until the Freethinkers have control.

Gentlemen, it isn't to have you think that I would call Christ "an illegitimate child", which hurts me: it is to think that you should think that I would think any the less of Christ if I knew it was so.

Who can account for the fact, if we are to be saved only by faith in Christ, that Matthew forgot it, that Luke said nothing about it, and that Mark never mentioned it except in two passages written by another person.

Christ said nothing about the Western Hemisphere because he did not know it existed. He did not know the shape of the earth. He was not a scientist—never even hinted at any science—never told anybody to investigate, to think. His idea was that this life should be spent in preparing for the next. For all of the evils of this life, and the next, faith was his remedy.

I have many objections to the philosophy of Christ. I do not believe in returning good for evil. I believe in returning justice for evil. I do not believe that I can put a man under a moral obligation to do me a favor by doing him a wrong. The doctrine of non-resistance is to me absurd. The right should be defended and the wrong resisted. Goodness should have the right to protect itself. Neither do I believe in decrying this world. We should not say, "Thou fool," to the man who works for those he loves. Poverty is not a virtue, nor is wealth a crime. Christ is not my ideal. Above any one man is humanity. (Letters)

I do not consider it a very important question whether Christ was the Son of God or not. After all, what difference does it make? If he never existed, we are under the same obligation to do what we believe is right; and believing that he was the Son of God or disbelieving it, is of no earthly importance. If we are ever judged at all it will be by our actions, and not by our beliefs. If Christ was good enough to die for me, he certainly

will not be bad enough to damn me for honestly failing to believe in his divinity. He will behave just as well in heaven as he
did while on earth; and certainly I should have no fear of the
fury of love and forgiveness. The only question is, am I honest?
(Letters)

Christianity (18th Century)

The Christianity of Paine's day is not the Christianity of our
time. There has been a great improvement since then. One hundred and fifty years ago the foremost preachers of our time
would have perished at the stake. A Universalist would have
been torn to pieces in England, Scotland and America. Unitarians would have found themselves in the stocks, pelted by the
rabble with dead cats, after which their ears would have been
cut off, their tongues bored and their foreheads branded.

Christianity (General)

The good part of Christianity—that is to say kindness, morality—will never go down. The cruel part ought to go down. And
by the cruel part I mean the doctrine of eternal punishment—of
allowing the good to suffer for the bad—allowing innocence to
pay the debt of guilt. So the foolish part of Christianity—that is
to say, the miraculous—will go down. The absurd part must
perish.

Christian Science

Question: Col., what about Christian Science?
    I think it is superstition, pure and unadulterated. I think
that soda will cure a sour stomach better than thinking. In my
judgement, quinine is a better tonic than meditation. If you can
absolutely control the body and all its functions by thought,
what is the use of buying coal? Let the mercury go down and
keep yourself hot by thinking. What is the use of wasting money
for food? Fill your stomach with think. According to these
Christian Science people all that really exists is an illusion, and
the only realities are things that don't exist.

Christmas, What I Want For

If I had the power to produce exactly what I want for next Christmas, I would have all the kings and emperors resign and allow the people to govern themselves.

I would have the nobility drop their titles and give their lands back to the people. I would have the Pope throw away his tiara and take off his sacred vestments, and admit that he is not acting for God—is not infallible—but is just an ordinary Italian. I would have all the cardinals, archbishops, bishops, priests, and clergymen admit that they know nothing about theology, nothing about hell or heaven, nothing about the destiny of the human race, nothing about devils or ghosts, gods or angels. I would have them tell their "flocks" to think for themselves, to be manly men and womanly women, and to do all in their power to increase the sum of human happiness.

I would have all the professors in colleges, all the teachers in schools of every kind, including those in Sunday schools, agree that they would teach only what they know, that they would not palm off guesses as demonstrated truths.

I would like to see all the editors of papers and magazines agree to print the truth and nothing but the truth, to avoid all slander and misrepresentation, and to let the private affairs of people alone.

I would like to see drunkenness and prohibition both abolished.

I would like to see corporal punishment done away with in every home, in every school, in every asylum, reformatory and prison. Cruelty hardens and degrades; kindness reforms and enobles.

I would like to see the millionaires unite and form a trust for the public good.

I would like to see a fair division of profits between capital and labor, so that the toiler could save enough to mingle a little June with the December of his life.

I would like to see an international court established in which to settle disputes between nations, so that armies could be disbanded and the great navies allowed to rust and rot in perfect peace.

I would like to see the whole world free—free from injustice—free from superstition.

This will do for next Christmas. The following Christmas, I may want more. (1897)

(The) Church and Money

When this verse was written, the church must have been nearly bankrupt. "It is easier for a camel to go through the eye of a needle than for a rich man to enter the kingdom of God." Did you ever know a wealthy disciple to unload on account of that verse?

The church taught obedience and faith—told the poor people that although they had a hard time here, working for nothing, they would be paid in Paradise with a large interest.

The church has always been willing to swap off treasures in heaven for cash down.

(The) Church and Segregation

In St. Louis the other day, I read an interview with a Christian minister—one who is now holding a revival. They call him the boy preacher—a name that he has borne for 50 or 60 years. The question was whether in these revivals when they were trying to rescue souls from eternal torture, they would allow colored people to occupy seats with white people. The revivalist preaching the unsearchable riches of Christ, said he would not allow the colored people to sit with the white people; they must go to the back of the church. These same Christians tell us that in heaven there will be no distinction; Christ cares nothing for the color of skin; in paradise white and black will sit together, swap harps, and cry hallelujah in chorus; yet this minister was not willing that a colored man should sit by a white man and hear the gospel of everlasting peace.

Church Building: Its Everyday Use

In this building should be the library of the town. It should be the clubhouse of the people, where they could find the principal newspapers and periodicals of the world. Its auditorium should be like a theater. Plays should be presented by home talent, an orchestra formed, music cultivated. The people should meet there at any time they desire. The women should carry their knitting and sewing and connected with it should be rooms for the playing of games, billiards, cards and chess. Everything should be as agreeable as possible. The citizens should take pride in this building. They should adorn its niches with statues and its walls with pictures. It should be the intellectual center. They should employ a gentleman of ability, possibly of genius to address them on Sundays, on subjects that would be of real interest, of real importance.

Editor's Note: It is entirely possible that many of the recommendations made by Ingersoll were based on his first-hand observation of what was going on at the People's Church in Kalamazoo. The comments were made just after his historic and favorable visit to People's.

Civil Rights

Editor's Note: All of the following quotes are taken from a speech delivered by Ingersoll, October 22, 1883, to an overflow crowd at Lincoln Hall, Washington, D.C. The U.S. Supreme Court had just declared unconstitutional a civil rights bill, not unlike that finally passed in 1964 following the death of John F. Kennedy.

In the struggle with England, our fathers justified their rebellion by declaring that Nature clothed all men with the right to life, liberty, and the pursuit of happiness. The moment that success crowned their efforts, they changed their noble declaration of equal rights for all, and basely interpolated the word "white". Our fathers planted the seeds of injustice and we gathered the harvest. In the blood and flame of civil war, we retraced our fathers' steps.

The first duty of the General Government is to protect each citizen. The first duty of each citizen is to be true—not to his state, but to the Republic.

If this is not now a free government; if citizens cannot now be protected, regardless of race or color; if the three sacred amendments (13, 14, & 15) have been undermined by the Supreme Court—we must have another; and if that fails, then another; and we must neither stop, nor pause, until the Constitution shall become a perfect shield for every right, of every human being, beneath our flag.

The government cannot shirk its responsibility by leaving a citizen to be protected in his rights, as a citizen of the U.S., by a state.

Do you wish to put the ballot box in the keeping of the shotgun, and of the White-Liners, of the Ku Klux? Do you wish to put the ballot box in the keeping of men who openly swear that they will not be ruled by a majority of American citizens if a portion of that majority is made of black men?

Any government which makes a distinction on account of color, is a disgrace to the age in which we live. The idea that a man like Frederick Douglass (Black U.S. Ambassador to Haiti) can be denied entrance to a car, that the doors of a hotel can be shut in his face; that he may be prevented from entering a theater—the idea that there shall be some ignominious corner into which such a man can be thrown by a decision of the Supreme Court! This idea is simply absurd.

The more political power the colored man has the better he will be treated. If he ever holds the balance of power he will be treated as well as the balance of our citizens. My idea is that the colored man should stand on an equality with the white before the law; that he should be allowed to vote, and that his vote should be counted. It is a simple question of honesty. The Colored people are doing well; they are industrious; they are trying to get an education, and on the whole, I think they are behaving fully as well as the whites. They are the most forgiving people in the world, and about the only real Christians in our country. They have suffered enough, and for one, I am on their side. I think more of honest black people than of dishonest whites, to say the least of it.

I make no distinction of race.

Virtue is of no color; kindness, justice and love of no complexion.

I pity the man who has only to brag that he is white.

It will not do in the second century of this nation to insult a man because of his nation(ality).

Conformity

Is it desirable that all should be exactly alike in their religious convictions? Religion tries to force all minds into one mold. Knowing they all cannot believe, the church endeavors to make them all say they believe. She longs for the unity of hypocrisy, and detests the splendid diversity of individuality and freedom.

X   Do not most people mistake for freedom the right to examine their own chains?

Custom meets us at the cradle and leaves us only at the tomb. Our first questions are answered by ignorance and our last by superstition.

To give up your individuality is to annihilate yourself.

We should all remember that to be like other people is to be unlike ourselves.

Nothing can be more detestable in character than servile imitation.

The individual is constantly counting for less.

Cooking

Cooking is one of the fine arts. Good cooking is the basis of civilization. There ought to be a law making it a crime, punishable by imprisonment to fry beefsteak. Broil it; it is just as easy, and when broiled it is delicious. Fried beefsteak is not fit for a wild beast.

Coxey's Army

Editor's Note: While Ingersoll did not sympathize with Coxey and his demands, he supported his right to speak, and thought the arrest of the Populist on the steps of the nation's Capitol a bad mistake, an injustice.

If they (Coxey's Army) had been rich, if they had gone to Washington in palace cars, they would have been allowed to parade and say their say.

Creeds

Most of the orthodox creeds were born of bad cooking. Bad food produced dyspepsia, and dyspepsia produced Calvinism and Calvinism is the cancer of Christianity. Oatmeal is responsible for the worst features of Scotch Presbyterianism. Half-cooked beans account for the religion of the Puritans. Fried bacon and saleratus biscuit underlie the doctrine of States' Rights. Lent is a mistake, fasting is a blunder, and bad cooking is a crime. If they (the Christians) think that there is some subtle relation between hunger and heaven, or that faith depends upon, or is strengthened by famine, or that veal during Lent is the enemy of virtue, or that beef breeds blasphemy while fish feeds faith, of course, all this means nothing to me.

If there is any dogma that ought to be protected by law, predestination is that doctrine. Surely, it is a cheerful, joyous thing, to one who is laboring, struggling, and suffering in this weary world, to think that before he existed, before the earth was, before a star had glittered in the heavens; before a ray of light had left the quiver of the sun, his destiny had been irrevocably fixed, and that for an eternity before his birth he had been doomed to bear eternal pain.

Does anybody believe the resurrection who has the courage to think for himself? Here is a man, for instance, who weighs 200 pounds and gets sick and dies weighing 120; how much will he weigh in the morning of the resurrection? Here is a cannibal who eats another man; we know that the atoms you

eat go into your body and become a part of you. After the cannibal has eaten the missionary, and appropriated his atoms to
himself, and then dies, to whom will the atoms belong in the
morning of the resurrection? Could the missionary maintain an
action of replevin, and if so, what would the cannibal do for a
body?

Creeds: The Trinity

Christ according to the faith, is the second person in the Trinity,
the Father being the first and the Holy Ghost the third. Each of
these three persons is God. Christ is his own father and his own
son. The Holy Ghost is neither father nor son, but both. The son
was begotten by the father, but existed before he was begotten—just the same before as after. Christ is just as old as his
father, and the father is just as young as his son. The Holy
Ghost proceeded from the Father and Son, but was an equal
to the Father and Son before he proceeded, that is to say before
he existed, but he is of the same age as the other two.

So it is declared that the Father is God, and the Son God,
and the Holy Ghost God, and that these three Gods make one
God.

According to the celestial multiplication table, once one is
three, and three times one is one, and according to heavenly
subtraction if we take two from three, three are left. The addition is equally peculiar. If we add two to one we have but one.
Each one is equal to himself and the other two.

How is it possible to prove the existence of the Trinity?

Nothing ever was, nothing ever can be more perfectly
idiotic and absurd than the dogma of the Trinity.

Think of one of these beings as the father of one, and think
of that one as half human and all God, and think of the third as
having proceeded from the other two, and then think of all
three as one. Think that after the father begat the son, the
father was still alone, and after the Holy Ghost proceeded from
the father and the son, the father was still alone—because there
never was and never will be but one God.

At this point, absurdity having reached its limit, nothing more can be said except: "Let us pray."

"Thou shalt not kill" is as old as life itself. And for this reason a large majority of people in all countries have objected to being murdered.

My own belief is the system in vogue now in regard to the treatment of criminals in many states produces more crime than it prevents.

Every creed is a rock in running water: humanity sweeps by it. Every creed cries to the universe, "Halt". A creed is the ignorant Past bullying the enlightened Present.

Crime and Punishment

The prisons are full; the courts are crowded, the officers of the law are busy, and there seems to be no material decrease in crime. It is impossible to make the penalty horrible enough to lessen crime. The criminal is dangerous and society has a right to protect itself. A penitentiary should be a school; the convicts should be educated. As it is now, there is but little reform. The same faces appear again and again at the bar.

Let us remember that criminals are produced by conditions, and let us do what we can to change the conditions and to reform the criminals.

If you want to stop crime you must treat it properly. The conditions of society must not be such as to produce criminals.

I regard criminals as unfortunates. Most people regard those who violate the law with hatred. Society has no right to take revenge; no right to torture a convict; no right to do wrong because some individual has done wrong. I am opposed to all corporal punishments in penitentiaries. I am opposed to anything that degrades a criminal.

Criminals have been flogged, mutilated, tortured in a thousand ways, and the only effect was to demoralize, harden, and degrade society and increase the number of crimes. In my judgement, no human being was ever made better, nobler by being whipped or clubbed.

Solitary confinement is a species of torture. I think the criminal should not be punished. He should be reformed, if he is capable of reformation.

Society should not punish; it should protect itself only.

Capital punishment degrades and hardens a community and it is the work of savagery. It is savagery. Capital punishment does not prevent murder, but sets an example—by the State—that is followed by its citizens. The State murders its enemies and the citizen murders his.

If the death penalty is to be inflicted, let it be done in the most humane way. For my part, I should like to see the criminal removed, if he must be removed, with the same care and with the same mercy that you would perform a surgical operation. Why inflict pain? Who wants it inflicted? What good can it, by any possibility, do? To inflict unnecessary pain hardens him who inflicts it, hardens each among those who witness it, and tends to demoralize the community.

I think the refusal of Governor Theodore Roosevelt to commute the sentence of Mrs. Place is a disgrace to the state. What a spectacle of a man killing a woman—taking a poor, pallid, and frightened woman, strapping her to a chair and then arranging the apparatus so she can be shocked to death. Many call this a Christian nation. A good many people who believe in hell would naturally feel it their duty to kill a wretched insane woman.

I understand that John G. Shortall, president of the Humane Society of Illinois, has had a bill introduced in to the Legislature of the state for the establishment of the whipping post. Nothing could be more infamous, and yet this man is President of the Humane Society. Now the question arises, what is humane about this society? Certainly not its president. Undoubtedly, he is sincere. Certainly no man would take that position unless he was sincere. Nobody deliberately pretends to be bad, but the idea of his being President of the Humane Society is simply preposterous. With his idea about the whipping post he might join a society of hyenas for the cultivation of ferocity, for certainly nothing short of that would do justice to his bill.

Death & Dying (See also Immortality, Suicide)

[**Question:** Col., what is worse than death?] Oh, a great many things. To be dishonored. To be worthless. To feel that you are a failure. To be insane. To be constantly afraid of the future. To lose the ones you love.

And suppose after all that death does end all. Next to eternal joy, next to being forever with those we love and those who loved us, next to that, is to be wrapt in the dreamless drapery of eternal peace. Next to eternal life is eternal sleep. Upon the shadowy shore of death the sea of trouble casts no wave. Eyes that have been curtained by the everlasting dark, will never know again the burning touch of tears. Lips touched by eternal silence will never speak again the broken words of grief. Hearts of dust do not break. The dead do not weep. Within the tomb no veiled and weeping sorrow sits, and in the rayless gloom is crouched no shuddering fear.

I had rather think of those I have loved and lost, as having returned to earth, as having become a part of the elemental wealth of the world. I would rather think of them as unconscious dust, I would rather dream of them as gurgling in the streams, floating in the clouds, bursting in the foam of light upon the shores of worlds. I would rather think of them as lost visions of a forgotten night, than to have the faintest fear that their naked souls have been clutched by an orthodox god. I will leave the dead where nature leaves them. Whatever flower of hope springs up in my heart I will cherish; I will give it breath of sighs and rain of tears. But I cannot believe that there is any being in this universe who has created a human soul for eternal pain.

I would rather that every God destroy himself; I would rather that we all should go to eternal chaos, to black and starless night, than that just one soul should suffer eternal agony.

What would you think of a man who built a railroad, knowing that every passenger was to be killed—knowing that there was no escape? What would you think of the cheerfulness of the passengers if every one knew that at some station, the name of which had not been called out, there was a hearse waiting for him; backed up there, horses fighting flies, driver whistling, waiting for you? Is it not wonderful that the passengers on that train really enjoy themselves? Is it not magnificent that every one of them, under perpetual sentence of death, after all, can dimple their cheeks with laughter; that we, every one doomed to become dust, can yet meet around this table as full of joy as spring is full of life, as full of hope as the heavens are full of stars? I tell you, we have got a good deal of pluck . . . Suppose that when you die it is the end. The last thing that you will know is that you are alive, and the last thing that will happen to you is the curtain, not falling, but the curtain rising on another thought, so that as far as your consciousness is concerned you will and must live forever. No man can remember when he commenced and no man can remember when he ends. As far as we are concerned we live both eternities, the one past and the one to come, and it is a delight to me to feel satisfied, and to feel in my heart that I can never be certain that I have seen the faces I love for the last time.

Design in the Universe

Design does not prove creation. You find the planets arranged in accordance with what you call a plan. That does not prove that they were created. It may prove that they are governed, but it certainly does not prove that they were created. Is it consistent to say that a design cannot exist without a designer but that a designer can? Does not a designer need a design as much as a design needs a designer? Does not a Creator need a Creator as much as the thing we think has been created?

Man in his ignorance supposed that all phenomena were produced by some intelligent powers with direct reference to him.

These religious people see nothing but design everywhere, and personal intelligent interference in everything. They insist that the universe has been created, and that the adaptation of means to ends is perfectly apparent. They point us to the sunshine, to the flowers, to the April rain, and to all there is of beauty and of use in the world. Did it ever occur to them that a cancer is as beautiful in its development as is the reddest rose? That what they are pleased to call the adaptation of means to ends, is as apparent in the cancer as in the April rain? How beautiful the process of digestion. By what ingenious methods the blood is poisoned so that the cancer shall have food! By what wonderful contrivances the entire system of man is made to pay tribute to this divine and charming cancer! What beautiful colors it presents! Seen through the microscope it is a miracle of order and beauty. All the ingenuity of man cannot stop its growth. Think of the amount of thought it must have required to invent a way by which the life of one man might be given to produce one cancer. Is it possible to look upon it and doubt that there is a design in the universe, and that the inventor of this wonderful cancer must be infinitely powerful, ingenious and good?

Nature is but an endless series of efficient causes. She cannot create but she eternally transforms. There was no beginning and there can be no end.

From Copernicus we learned that this earth is only a grain of sand on the infinite shore of the universe; that everywhere we are surrounded by shining worlds vastly greater than our own, all moving and existing in accordance with law. True, the earth began to grow small, but man began to grow great.

Can we find "design" in the fact that every animal lives upon some other—that every drop of every sea is a battlefield where the strong devours the weak? Over the precipice of cruelty rolls a perpetual Niagara of blood. Is there "design" in this?

This grain of sand and tear they call the earth is the only world I have ever lived in. And you have no idea how little I know about the rest of this universe. You will never know how little I know about it until you examine your own minds on the subject. The plan is this: Life feeds on life. Justice does not always triumph. Innocence is not a perfect shield.

Divorce (See also Woman & Marriage)

Editor's Note: A New Jersey housewife suffered the horror of having her eyes torn out of their sockets by her enraged husband. The theological question of the hour was whether she should be able to obtain a divorce from this fiend. Ingersoll replied to a reporter's inquiry concerning his attitude on divorce.

Yes, I read the account, and I don't remember of ever having read anything more perfectly horrible or cruel. It is impossible for me to imagine such a monster, or to account for such an inhuman human being. How a man could deprive a human being of sight, except where some religious question is involved, is beyond my comprehension. When we take into consideration the crime of the man who blinded his wife, it is impossible NOT to think of the right of divorce. Must a woman in order to retain her womanhood become a slave, a serf, with a wild beast for a master. Has not the married woman the right of self-defense?

When the civilized man finds his wife loves another he does not kill, he does not murder. He says to his wife, "You are free." When the civilized woman finds that her husband loves another, she does not kill, she does not murder. She says to her husband, "I am free."

In some states the husband can obtain a divorce on the ground that his wife has committed adultery, but the wife cannot secure a divorce from the husband simply for the reason that he has been guilty of the same offence. The idea that marriage is something more than a contract is at the bottom of the legal and judicial absurdities that surround this subject. Whom Nature hath put asunder let not man bind and manacle together.

Is it in the interest of society that those who despise each other should live together? Can anything be more infamous than for a government to compel a woman to remain the wife of a man she hates—of one whom she justly holds in abhorrence? Must this woman, full of kindness, affection, healthy, be tied and chained to this living corpse?

Most of the laws about divorce are absurd or cruel and ought to be repealed.

Due Process of Law (See also Haymarket Square)

I do wish that every law providing for the punishment of a criminal offense should distinctly define the offense. That is the objection to this (Comstock) law, that it does not define the offense, so that an American citizen can readily know when he is about to break it and consequently the law, in all probability, is to be modified in that regard. I am in favor of every law defining with perfect distinctness the offense to be punished. This obscene law is a stumbling block.

The worst form of anarchy is when a judge violates his conscience and bows to popular demand. A court should care nothing for public opinion. An honest judge decides the law, not as it ought to be, but as it is, and the state of the public mind throws no light upon the question of what the law then is. But no matter how bad a man is, he has the right to be fairly tried. If he cannot be fairly tried, then there is anarchy on the bench. So I was opposed to the execution of those men. In my judgement a great mistake was made. I am on the side of mercy, and if I ever make mistakes, I hope they will all be made on that side. I have not the slightest sympathy with the feeling of revenge. Neither have I ever admitted, and I never shall, that every citizen has not the right to give his opinion on all that may be done by any servant of the people, by any judge, or by a court, by an officer—however small or however great. Each man in the U.S. is a sovereign and a king can freely speak his mind.

Ecological Concern

The destruction of game and of singing birds is to be regretted greatly, not only in this country but in all others. The people of America have been too busy felling forests, ploughing fields, and building houses, to cultivate to the highest degree, the aesthetic side of their nature.

It is true that seal fisheries are being destroyed in the interest of the present, by those who care nothing for the future. All these things are to be deprecated, are to be spoken against.

Education

I believe that education is the only lever capable of raising mankind. If we wish to make the future of the Republic glorious we must educate the children of the present. The greatest blessing conferred by our government is the free school. In importance it rises above everything else that government does. In its influence it is far greater.

There is no real reforming power in fear or punishment. Men cannot be tortured into greatness, into goodness. In the atmosphere of kindness the seed of virtue bursts into bud and flower.

The object of all education should be to increase the usefulness of man—usefulness to himself and to others. Every human being should be taught that his first duty is to take care of himself, and that to be self-respecting he must be self-supporting. To live on the labor of others, either by force which enslaves, or by cunning which robs, or by borrowing or begging, is wholly dishonorable. Every man should be taught some useful art. His hands should be educated as well as his head. He should be taught to deal with things as they are—with life as it is. This would give a feeling of independence which is the firmest foundation of honor, of character. Every man knowing he is useful admires himself.

The great trouble with the public school is that many things are taught that are of no immediate use. I believe in manual training schools. I believe in the kindergarten system. Every person ought to be taught to do something—ought to be taught the use of their hands.

Editor's Note: When Ingersoll visited People's Church in Kalamazoo, 1896, he became aware of the first public kindergarten in the State of Michigan. Daily the church basement hosted the kindergarten.

The more real education, the less crime—the more homes, the fewer prisons.

The a,b,c's are the breastworks of human liberty—free schools for the education of all the children in the land.

The common school is the breath of life.

I regard the public school as the bread of life.

Teachers are poorly paid; only the best should be employed.

The most significant fact in the world today, is, that in nearly every village under the American flag, the schoolhouse is larger than the church.

Too much doubt is better than too much credulity.

The gymnast or athlete should seek for health as the student should seek for truth, but when the athletics degenerate into mere personal contests, they become dangerous, because the contestants lose sight of health.

Most of the colleges of this country have simply classified ignorance.

Every child should be taught to doubt, to inquire, to demand reasons.

For the most part, colleges are places where pebbles are polished and diamonds are dimmed.

Ignorance is the mother of mystery and misery, of superstition and sorrow, of waste and want.

As long as man lives he should study. Death alone has the right to dismiss the school. No man can get too much knowledge.

Evolution

When I first heard of that doctrine, I did not like it. My heart was filled with sympathy for those people who have nothing to be proud of except ancestors. I thought how terrible this will be upon the nobility of the Old World. Think of their being forced to trace their ancestry back to the duke Orang Outang, or to the princess Chimpanzee. After thinking it over, I came to the conclusion that I liked that doctrine.

Faith

Faith reigned with scarcely a rebellious subject . . . She built cathedrals for God and dungeons for men. She peopled the clouds with angels and the earth with slaves.

Abject faith is barbarism; reason is civilization. To obey is slavish; to act from a sense of obligation perceived by reason is noble. Ignorance worships mystery; reason explains it; the one grovels, the other soars. Is it possible to flatter God by pretending to believe, or by believing, that which is repugnant to reason, that which upon examination is seen to be absurd?

Falsehoods

Many people imagine that falsehoods may become respectable on account of age, that a certain reverence goes with antiquity, and that if a mistake is covered with the moss of sentiment it is altogether more credible than a parvenu fact. They endeavor to introduce the idea of aristocracy into the world of thought, believing and honestly, believing that a falsehood long believed is far superior to a truth that is generally denied.

A lie will not fit a fact. It will only fit another lie made for the purpose. The life of a lie is simply a question of time. Nothing but truth is immortal.

Freedom of Conscience

The combined wisdom and genius of all mankind cannot possibly conceive of an argument against liberty of thought.

There is this difference between thought and action: for our actions we are responsible to ourselves and to those injuriously affected. For thoughts there can, in the nature of things, be no responsibility to gods or men, here or hereafter.

Society demands that either you belong to some church or that you suppress your opinions.

True religion must be free. Without perfect liberty of mind there can be no true religion. Without liberty the brain is a dungeon—the mind a convict.

Nothing can be more infamous than intellectual tyranny. To put chains upon the body is nothing compared with putting shackles on the brain. No god is entitled to the worship or respect of a man who does not give, even to the meanest of his children, every right he claims for himself. If the Pentateuch is true, religious persecution is a duty. The dungeons of the Inquisition were temples and the clank of every chain upon the limbs of heresy was music to the ear of God.

Intellectual liberty is the air of the soul, the sunshine of the mind, and without it, the world is a prison; the universe is a dungeon.

A Christian who does not believe in absolute intellectual liberty is a curse to mankind. An Infidel who does believe in absolute intellectual liberty is a blessing to this world. We cannot expect all infidels to be good, nor all Christians bad, and we might make some mistakes even if we selected these people ourselves. I never did pretend that the fact that a man was a Christian ever tended to show that he was a bad man. Neither have I insisted that the fact that a man is an Infidel even tends to show what, in other respects, his character is.

I have made up my mind that no necessity of bread, or roof, or raiment shall ever put a padlock on my lips. I have made up my mind that no hope of preferment, no honor, no wealth, shall ever make me for one moment swerve from what I really believe, no matter whether it is to my immediate interest, as one would think or not. And while I live, I am going to do what little I can to help my fellow men who have not been as fortunate as I have been. I shall talk on their side. I shall vote on their side.

Garden of Eden

The Garden of Eden is always behind us. The Golden Age, after all, is the memory of youth—it is the result of remembered pleasure in the midst of present pain.

Banish me from Eden when you will; but first let me eat of the fruit of the tree of knowledge.

Is there an intelligent man or woman in the world who now believes the Garden of Eden story? If you find any man who believes it, strike his forehead and you will hear an echo. Something is for rent.

God/Gods

Each nation has created a god, and the god has always resembled his creators. He hated and loved what they hated and loved, and he was invariably found on the side of those in power. Each god was intensely patriotic, and detested all nations but his own.

None of these gods could give a true account of the creation of this little earth. All were woefully deficient in geology and astronomy. As a rule they were most miserable legislators, and as executives they were far inferior to the average of American presidents.

No god was ever in advance of the nation that created him. The Negroes represented their deities with black skins and curly hair. The Mongolians gave to theirs a yellow complexion and dark almond-shaped eyes.

There may be a God who will make us happy in another world. If he does, it will be more than he has accomplished in this. A being who has the power to prevent it and yet allows thousands and millions of his children to starve, who devours them with earthquakes, who allows whole nations to be enslaved, cannot—in my judgement—be implicitly depended upon to do justice in another world.

Strange! that no one has ever been persecuted by the church for believing God bad, while hundreds of millions have been destroyed for thinking him good. The orthodox church will never forgive the Universalist for saying, "God is love." It has always been considered one of the very highest evidences of true and undefiled religion that all men, women and children deserve eternal damnation. It has always been heresy to say, "God will at last save all."

God improves as man advances.

Jehovah was not a moral God. He had all the vices and he lacked all the virtues. He generally carried out all his threats, but he never faithfully kept a promise.

Man has never been at a loss for gods.

God may have changed his mind on many things. He has on slavery and polygamy at least, according to the church. Yet his church now wants to go and destroy polygamy in Utah with the sword. Why do they not send missionaries there with copies of the Old Testament? By reading the lives of Abraham, Isaac and Lot and a few other patriarchs who ought to have been in the penitentiary, maybe they can soften their hearts.

If God governs this world, if he builds and destroys, if back of every event is his will, then he is neither good nor wise. He is ignorant and malicious. A few days ago, in Paris, men and women gathered together in the name of Charity. The building in which they were assembled took fire and many of these men and women perished in the flames. A French priest called this horror an act of God. Is it not strange that Christians speak of their God as an assassin?

If there is a God who has allowed the children to be oppressed in this world he certainly needs another life to reform the blunders he made in this.

Admitting that a god did create the universe, the question then arises, of what did he create it? It certainly was not made of nothing. Nothing, considered in the light of a raw material, is a decided failure.

Special providence is a mistake.

The universe is all the God there is.

I am as much opposed to an autocrat hereafter as now.

God so loved the world that he made up his mind to damn a large majority of the human race.

Some people say that God existed from eternity, and has created eternity. It is impossible to conceive of an act co-equal with eternity. If you say that God has existed forever, and has always acted, then you make the universe as old as God. If the universe is as old as God, he certainly did not create it! These questions of origin and destiny—of infinite gods—are beyond the powers of the human mind. They cannot be solved. We might as well try to travel fast enough to get beyond the horizon. It is like a man trying to run away from his girdle.

Our ignorance is God; what we know is science.

The government of God was tried in Geneva when John Calvin was his representative. Under this government of God, the flames climbed around the limbs and blinded the eyes of Michael Servetus, because he dared to express an honest thought. This government of God was established in New England and the result was that Quakers were hanged or burned. This government of God was established in Spain, and the Jews were expelled. This government of God was tried in the U.S. when slavery was regarded as a divine institution. The pulpit of that day defended the buying and selling of women and babes. The mouths of the slave-traders were filled with passages of Scripture, defending and upholding traffic in human flesh.

Is it not strange that God, though he gave hundreds of directions for the purpose of discovering the presence of leprosy, and for cleansing the leper after he was healed, forgot to tell how the disease could be cured? Is it not wonderful that while God told his people what animals were fit for food he failed to give a list of plants that man might eat? Why did he leave his children to find out the hurtful and the poisonous by experiment, knowing that experiment in millions of cases, must be death?

The fact is, we have no national religion and no national God. Every citizen is allowed to have a religion and a God of his own, or to reject all religions and deny the existence of all gods.

God cannot send to eternal pain a man who has done something toward improving the condition of his fellow-man. If he can, I had rather go to hell than to heaven and keep company with such a god.

An honest God is the noblest work of man.

There is nothing a man can do for God, as God needs nothing. But there are many things we can do for our fellowmen because many of them are in constant need. All days should be for the good of man, and that day in which the most people are really happy, is the best day. (Letters)

I do not say there is no God. I do not know. As I told you before, I have travelled but very little—only in this world.

Government

The government has no right to invade the privacy of a citizen.

There is but one use for law, but one excuse for government—the preservation of liberty.

The principal object of all government should be to protect those in the right from those in the wrong. There is a vast number of people who need to be protected who are unable, by reason of the defects in their minds and by the countless circumstances that enter into the question of making a living, to protect themselves.

That is a wretched government where the honest and the industrious beg, unsuccessfully for the right to toil; where those who are willing, anxious, and able to work, cannot get bread. If everything is to be left to the blind and heartless working of the laws of supply and demand, why have governments? If the nation leaves the poor to starve, and the weak and unfortunate to perish, it is hard to see for what purpose the nation should be preserved. If our statesmen are not wise enough to foster great enterprises, and to adopt a policy that will give us prosperity, it may be that the laboring classes, driven to frenzy by hunger, the bitterness of which will be increased by seeing others in the midst of plenty, will seek remedy in destruction.

Until all nations submit their differences to an international court—a court with the power to carry its judgement into effect by having the armies and navies of the world pledged to support it—the world will not be civilized.

I believe that this is a nation. I believe in the equality of all men before the law, irrespective of race, religion, or color. I believe that there should be a dollar's worth of silver in the silver dollar. I believe in a free ballot and a fair count. I believe in protecting those industries and only those that need protection. I believe in the unrestricted coinage of gold and silver. I believe in the rights of the State, the rights of the citizens, and the sovereignty of the nation. I believe in the unqualified and absolute liberty of thought.

I am an individualist instead of a Socialist. I am a believer in individuality and in each individual taking care of himself. I want the government to do just as little as it can consistently with the safety of the nation. I want as little law as possible. But if a government gives privileges to the few, the few must not oppress the many. The government has no right to bestow any privilege upon any man or corporation, except for the public good. That which is a special privilege to the few should be a special benefit to the many. I do not pretend to know enough to suggest a remedy for all the evils of society. While I may not believe a certain theory will work, still, if I feel sure that it will do no harm, I am willing to see it tried. I am in sympathy with the laboring men of all kinds, whether they labor with hands or brain. If the object of the laboring men is to improve their conditions without injuring others, to become prosperous and civilized, I sympathize with them and hope they will succeed. I have not the slightest sympathy with those that wish to accomplish all these objects through brute force. I have sometimes thought that I should like to see the laboring men in power, so that they could realize how little, after all, can be done by law. Personally, I am for the abolition of all special privileges that are not for the general good.

I know that you desire to make your fellow creatures happy. I am perfectly aware of that. But the great question is, can you control people who cannot or will not control themselves? There is still another question, will men who will not work for themselves willingly work for others? (ISH Letter to Eugene V. Debs)

We must welcome to our shores the exiles of the world, nd we may not drive them back. Some may be deformed by hunger, broken in spirit, victims of tyranny and caste—in whose sad faces may be read the touching record of a weary life—and yet their children, born of liberty and love will be symmetrical and fair, intelligent and free. (ISH fragment)

We want man to rule this world. (ISH notes)

I believe in protecting American industries but I do not believe in rocking the cradle when the infant is seven feet tall and wears a number twelve shoe. (ISH papers)

The way to stop gambling in a city like this (NYC) is to have it absolutely open and prevent any gambling in secret. It will not do one-tenth the harm. There is more money lost and won on the produce exchanges, the stock exchanges, the cotton exchanges, all of which is pure gambling—in one year—than has been lost and won on all the cards ever played or in all the devices ever invented since the birth of history. To leave these great exchanges in full blast and grab a fellow and chuck him in jail because he has wagered 50ᶜ on three kings seems, to me, to be a little idiotic. (ISH papers)

I think the question of States' Rights is dead, except that it can be used to defeat the democracy. It is what might be called a convenient political corpse. (1879)

There is no nation in which the majority leads the way. In the progress of man, the few have been the nearest right. Wisdom has often been trampled beneath the feet of the multitude. To help others help themselves is the only real charity.

If the Legislature of New York would re-enact next winter the Mosaic code, the members might consider themselves lucky if they were not hung upon their return home.

I think it somewhat dangerous to deprive even one American citizen of the right to govern himself.

The Supreme Court of Illinois has just made a good decision. The Court decided that a contract made on Sunday can be enforced. In other words, that Sunday is not holy enough to sanctify a fraud.

We have a king here and that king is the law. We all stand equal before that law. Government cannot by law create wealth. The government produces nothing.

Nothing is farther from democracy than this perpetual application of the veto power. As a matter of fact, it should be abolished, and the utmost a President should be allowed to do, would be to return a bill with his objections, and the bill should then become law on being passed by both houses by a simple majority. This would give the Executive the opportunity of calling attention to the supposed defects and getting the judgement of Congress a second time.

I suppose that the superstition most prevalent with public men, is the idea that they are of great importance to the public. Men in office reflect the average intelligence of the people, and no more.

Judges keep their backs to the dawn.

I have no objection to a third term on principle or for that matter a fourth term.

Socialism seems to be the worst form of slavery.

Intelligence, integrity and courage are the great pillars that support the state.

The taxes in this country are paid by labor and industry. They should be collected and disbursed by integrity.

So I believe in cumulative taxation with regard to any kind of wealth. Let a man worth ten million dollars pay a greater percent than one worth 100,000 because he is able to pay it. The other day a man was talking to me about having the dead pay the expenses of government. Whenever a man dies worth, say, five million dollars, one million should go to the government. If he died worth ten million, three million should go to the government. If he died worth twenty million dollars, eight million should go to the government and so on. I should be in favor of cumulative taxation upon legacies—the greater the legacy, the greater the percent of the taxation.

I hope the time will come when the government will give as much to educate two men as to kill one. (1881)

Grammercy Park Residence Memorial Plaque, 1925

Editor's Note: In 1925, the Grammercy Park Hotel opened its doors to the public. It had been built on the site of the Ingersoll residence. A group of the Great Agnostic's admirers asked the hotel for permission to place a plaque commemorating the fact of Ingersoll's residence having been at 52 Grammercy Park, now occupied by the hotel. Many distinguished citizens were present to participate in the ceremony. The Program Committee included such notables as Luther Burbank, Thomas Edison, Hamlin Garland, Margaret Sanger, Heywood Broun, Carrie Chapman Catt, Zona Gale, Edwin Markham, Edgar Lee Masters, David S. Muzzey, Albert Bigelow, James Harvey Robinson, Charles Edward Russell and Lorado Taft. (ISH Col.) Edgar Lee Masters read the following poem which he had written for the occasion:

Men build them houses and soon the unbidden guest
Enters, and then the houses are pulled down.
Houses are only blossoms, and winter comes
To them and frosts their summer time's renown.

As if to stay the glacier's ruthless hand
We mark with bronze the place of vanished walls
Of houses famed. But with the passing years
The city changes and the tablet falls.

All passes of memorials which would sound
The triumphs of the voice or of the pen,
Which need them not. Serenely they have found
A lasting dwelling in the minds of men

Who spring as temples of living memory
Wherever thought and hope and progress stir,
Until the eternal mountains are their bronze
And all the earth their lasting sepulchre.

The house that stood here vanished, and in time
Nothing shall be here of this newer wall,
Save Memory that once again may come
To mark this entrance spot of Ingersoll.

But if Time lose the doorway where his feet
Sounded their earthly entrance, still the key
Of his entering thought will wake the hospitable mind
To welcome him and the wanderer Liberty.

November 9th, 1925

Haymarket Square and the Chicago "Anarchists"

These men were convicted during a period of great excite-
ment—tried when the press demanded their conviction—when
it was asserted that society was on the edge of destruction unless these men were hanged. The judge instructed the jury to
the effect that where men have talked in a certain way, and
where the jury believed that the result of such talk might be the
commission of a crime, that such men are responsible for that
crime. Of course, there is neither law nor sense in instruction
like that. I hold that it must have been the intention of the man
making the remark; it must have been his intention that the
crime should be committed. I am satisfied that the defendant
Fielden never intended to harm a human being. As a matter of
fact, the evidence shows he was making a speech in favor of
peace at the time of the occurrence.

The Supreme Court of Illinois seems to have admitted that
the (Judge's) instruction was wrong, but took the ground that it
made no difference with the verdict. This is a dangerous course
for the court of last resort to pursue, neither is it very compli-

mentary to the judge who tried the case, that his instructions had no effect upon the jury.

There is no place in this country for the Anarchist. The source of power here is the people. The men who work for their living are the very men who have the power to make every law that is made in the U.S. They are in a majority.

Heaven

No one pretends to know where "heaven" is. The celestial realm is the blessed somewhere in the unknown nowhere.

The Rev. Mr. Spurgeon stated in a sermon that some people wondered what they would do through all eternity in Heaven. He said, that, as for himself, for the first one hundred thousand years he would look at the wound in one of the Savior's feet, and for the next one hundred thousand years he would look at the wound in his other foot, and for the next one hundred thousand years he would look at the wound in one of his hands and for the next one hundred thousand years he would look at the wound in the other hand, and for the next one hundred thousand years he would look at the wound in his side.

Surely, nothing could be more delightful than this. A man capable of being happy in such employment, could of course take great delight in reading even the genealogies of the Old Testament.

I have received yours of Feb. 16, in which you say that you want to meet me in Heaven. You certainly will if you are there. (Letters)

If only Christians go to heaven and all others go to hell, it seems to me that there will be a thousand times more misery in the next world or state than in this. (ISH Col.)

Hell

The doctrine of eternal punishment is the most infamous of all doctrines—born of ignorance, cruelty and fear. Around the angel of immortality Christianity has coiled the serpent. Upon Love's breast the church has placed the eternal asp.

I have denied with all my might, a great many times, the infamous doctrine of eternal punishment.

Editor's Note: No attitude is expressed more often by R.G.I. than this unremitting hatred for the doctrine of Hell. This is but one of hundreds of references to this horror.

Holidays

For my part I am willing to have two or three a year—the more holidays the better. Many people have an idea that I am opposed to Sunday. I am perfectly willing to have two a week. All I insist on is that these days shall be for the benefit of the people, and that they shall be kept in a way not to make folks miserable or sad or hungry, but in a way to make people happy, and to add a little to the joy of life. Of course, I am in favor of everybody keeping holidays to suit himself, provided he does not interfere with others, and I am perfectly willing that everybody should go to church on that day, provided he is willing that I should go somewhere else.

Hospitals and Health Care

I find that it is sometimes very difficult to get an injured man, or one seized with a sudden illness, taken into a city hospital. There are so many rules and so many regulations, so many things necessary to be done, that while the rules are being complied with, the soul of the sick or injured man, weary of the waiting, takes its flight. And, after the man is dead, the doctors are kind enough to certify that he died of heart failure . . . I do not think that hospitals should be places for young doctors to practice sawing off arms and legs of paupers or hunting in the stomachs of old women for tumors. I think only the skillful and the experienced should be employed in such places. Neither do I think hospitals should be places where medicine is distributed by students to the poor . . . I think every hospital, every asylum, every home for waifs and orphans should be supported by taxation, not by charity; should be under the care and control of the state absolutely. I do not believe in any institutions being managed by ANY INDIVIDUAL, or by any society, religious or secular, but by the state. I would no more have hospitals and asylums depend on charity than I would have the public schools depend on voluntary contributions . . . And let us do away forever with the idea that to care for the sick, for the helpless is charity. It is not a charity. It is a duty. It is something to be done for our own sakes. It is no more a charity than it is to pave or light the streets, no more charity than it is to have a system of sewers. It is all for the purpose of protecting society and of civilizing ourselves.

Immortality

Somebody asked Confucius about another world, and his reply was: "How should I know anything about another world when I know so little of this?"

Immortality is a word that Hope through all the ages has been whispering to Love. All hope to meet again the loved and lost. The miracle of thought we cannot understand. The mystery of life and death we cannot comprehend. This chaos called the world has never been explained. The golden bridge of life from gloom emerges and on shadow rests. Beyond this we do not know. Fate is speechless, destiny is dumb, and the secret of the future has never yet been told. We love; we wait; we hope. The more we love the more we fear. Upon the tenderest heart the deepest shadows fall. All paths whether filled with thorns or flowers end here. Here success and failure are the same. The rag of wretchedness and the purple robe of power all difference and distinction lose in this democracy of death. Character survives; goodness lives; love is immortal.

And yet to all a time may come when the fevered lips of life will long for the cool, delicious kiss of death—when tired of the dust and glare of day we shall hear with joy the rustling garments of the night. Let us believe that over the cradle Nature bends and smiles, and lovingly above the dead in benediction holds her outstretched hands.

Life is a narrow vale between the cold and barren peaks of two eternities. We strive to look beyond the heights. We cry aloud, and the only answer is the echo of our wailing cry. From the voiceless lips of the unreplying dead there comes no word; but in the night of death hope sees a star and listening, love can hear the rustle of a wing.

I do not say that man is not immortal. All I say is that there is no evidence that he lives again, and no demonstrations that we do not. It is better to ignorantly hope than to dishonestly affirm. (ISH unpublished lecture notes)

Without assurance and without fear, we give him back to Nature, the source and mother of us all.

Good deeds are never childless. A noble life is never lost. A virtuous action does not die.

New friends can never fill the places of the old.

Farewell, dear friend. The world is better for your life; the world is braver for your death. Farewell! We loved you living, and we love you now. A noble life enriches all the world.

In the very May of life another heart has ceased to beat. Night has fallen upon noon. But he lived, he loved, he was loved. Wife and children pressed their kisses on his lips. This is enough. The longest life contains no more. This fills the vase of joy.

The only thing that makes life endurable in this world is human love, and yet, according to Christianity, that is the very thing that we are not to have in the other world. We are to be so taken up with Jesus and angels, that we shall care nothing about our brothers and sisters that have been damned. We shall be so carried away with the music of the harp that we shall not even hear the wail of father or mother. Such a religion is a disgrace to human nature.

Man continually seeks to better his condition—not because he is immortal—but because he is capable of grief and pain, because he seeks for happiness.

I do not fear death any more than I fear sleep.

If we are immortal, it is a fact of nature, and that fact does not depend on bibles, on Christs, priests, or creeds.

I live, and that of itself is infinitely wonderful. It is no more wonderful that I may be again, if I have been, than that I am, having once been nothing.

I do not know which is better—life or death. It may be that death is the greatest gift that ever came from nature's open hand. We do not know.

Many people imagine that immortality must be an infinite good, but, after all, there is something terrible in the idea of an endless life. Think of a river that never reaches the sea, of a bird that never folds its wings, of a journey that never ends. I would rather be annihilated than to be an angel, with all the privileges of heaven, and yet have within my breast a heart that could be happy while those who have loved me in this world were in perdition.

The hope of immortality never came from any religion. That hope of immortality has helped to make religion.

I suppose that I believe that the atoms that are in me have been in many other people and in many other forms of life, and I suppose at death the atoms forming my body go back to the earth and are used in countless forms. These facts, or what I suppose to be facts, render a belief in the resurrection of the body impossible to me.

Indians

It is true that the Indians have been treated badly. It is true that the fringe of civilization has been composed of many low and cruel men. It is true that the red man has been demoralized by the vices of the white. It is a frightful fact that, when a superior race meets an inferior, the inferior imitates only the vices of the superior, and the superior those of the inferior. They exchange faults and failings. This is one of the most terrible facts in the history of the human race. Nothing can be said to justify our treatment of the Indians.

Jews

We should be grand enough and great enough to know that the rights of the Jews are precisely the same as our own. We cannot trample upon their rights without endangering our own; and no man who will take liberty from another, is great enough to enjoy liberty himself. Day by day Christians are laying the foundations of future persecution. In every Sunday School, little children are taught that Jews killed the God of this universe. Their little hearts are filled with hatred against the Jewish people. They are taught as a part of their creed to despise the descendants of the only people with whom God is ever said to have had any conversation whatever. When we take into consideration what the Jewish people have suffered, it is amazing that every one of them does not hate with all his heart and soul and strength the entire Christian world. But in spite of the persecutions they have endured, they are today, the most prosperous people on the globe . . .

If you wish to see the difference between some Jews and some Christians, compare the addresses of Felix Adler with the sermons of Mr. Talmadge.

Bismarck opposed a bill to do away with the disabilities of the Jews on the ground that Prussia is a Christian nation, founded for the purpose of spreading the gospel of Jesus Christ. I presume that it was his hatred of the Jews that caused him to return the resolutions. Bismarck should have lived several centuries ago. He belongs to the Dark Ages. He is a believer in the sword and the bayonet—in brute force.

The history of their (the Jews') persecution is, in my judgement, the saddest and the most infamous in the world.

I am utterly opposed to the oppression of any class, and regard the action of the proprietors of the Manhattan Beach Hotel in reference to Jews as bigoted, mean and disgraceful. Such action belongs to the Dark Ages. The persecution of the Jews should bring a blush to every Christian cheek. Nothing is more infamous than the oppression of a class. Each man has the right to be judged upon his own merits. To oppress him, or to hold him in contempt on account of religion, race, or color is a crime. Every man should be treated justly and kindly not because he is, or is not a Jew, or a Gentile, but because he is a human being, and, as such capable of joy or pain.

Joy and Laughter

Laughing has always been considered by theologians as a crime. Ministers have always said you will have no respect for our ideas unless you are solemn. Solemnity is a condition precedent to believing anything without evidence. And if you can only get a man solemn enough, awed enough, he will believe anything.

Why should we postpone our joy to another world? Thousands of people take great pleasure in dancing, and I say, let them dance. Dancing is better than weeping and wailing over a theology born of ignorance and superstition. And so with games of chance. There is a certain pleasure in playing games, and the pleasure is of the most innocent character. Let all these games be played at home and the children will not prefer the saloon to the society of their parents. I believe in cards and billiards. No one should fail to pick up every jewel of joy that can be found in his path. Every person should be as happy as he can provided he is not happy at the expense of another. Let us get all we can of the good between the cradle and the grave, all that we can of the truly dramatic, all that we can of enjoyment. If, when death comes, that is the end, we have at least made the best of this life. If there be another life, let us make the best of that.

Laughter is the blessed boundary line between brute and man. All blessings on the man who first gave the common air the music of laughter—the music that for the moment drove fears from the heart, tears from the eyes, and dimpled cheeks with joy.

In the vase of joy we find some tears.

Joy is wealth and love is the legal tender of the soul.

Humor is one of the most valuable things in the human brain. It is the torch of the mind—it sheds light. Humor is the readiest test of truth—of the natural, of the sensible—and when you take from a man all sense of humor there will only be enough left to make a bigot.

Labor and Capital

Every one should be taught the nobility of labor, the heroism and splendor of honest effort. As long as it is considered disgraceful to labor, or aristocratic not to labor, the world will be filled with idleness and crime, and with every possible moral deformity.

I sympathize with every honest effort made by the children of labor to improve their condition. That is a poorly governed country in which those who do the most have the least.

The men who cultivate the earth should own it.

When those who do the work own the machines, when those who toil control the invention, then, and not until then can the world be civilized and free. When these forces shall do the bidding of the individual, when they become the property of the mechanic instead of the monopoly, when they belong to labor instead of what is called capital, when these great powers are as free to the individual laborer as the air and light are now free to all, then—and not until then, the individual will be restored and all forms of slavery will disappear.

Will the workers always be ignorant enough and stupid enough to give their earnings for the useless? Will they support millions of soldiers to kill the sons of other workingmen? Will they learn that force to succeed, must have a thought behind it, and that anything done, in order that it may endure, must rest upon the corner-stone of justice?

We shall finally say that human flesh, human labor, shall not depend entirely on "supply and demand". That is infinitely cruel. Every man should give to another according to his ability to give—and enough that he may make his living and lay something by for the winter of old age.

What would you think of a man who had one thousand neckties, lying awake nights contriving how he might add one more to his collection? (I. Newton Baker)

The working people should be protected by law; if they are not the capitalists will require just as many hours as human nature will bear. We have seen here in America street-car drivers working sixteen and seventeen hours a day. It was necessary to have a strike to get fourteen, another strike to get twelve, and nobody could blame them for keeping on striking until they get to eight hours.

The free school in this country has tended to put men on an equality, and the mechanic understands his side of the case, and is able to express his views. Under these circumstances there must be a revolution. That is to say, the relations between capital and labor must be changed, and the time must come when they who do the work—they who make the money—will insist on having some of the profits.

I do not expect this remedy to come entirely from the government, or from government interference. I think the government can aid in passing good and wholesome laws—laws fixing the length of a labor day; laws preventing the employment of children; laws for the safety and security of the workingmen in mines and other dangerous places. But the laboring people must rely upon themselves; on their intelligence, and especially on their political power. They are the majority in this country. They can if they wish—if they stand together—elect

Congresses and Senates, Presidents and Judges. They have it in their power to administer the government of the U.S.

The laboring man, however, ought to remember that all who labor are their brothers, and that all the women who labor are their sisters and whenever one class of workingmen or workingwomen is oppressed all the other laborers ought to stand by the oppressed class. Probably the worst paid people in the world are the workingwomen . . . I would like to see all the working people unite for the purpose of demanding justice not only for men but for women.

I hope the time will come when labor receives far more than it does today (1888). I want you all to think of it—how little, after all, the laboring man receives. There is no place in the whole wide world where, in my judgement, labor reaps its true reward. There never has been. But I hope the time will come when the American laborer will not only make a living for himself, his wife, and children, but lay aside something to keep the roof above his head when the winter of age may come. I would rather see thousands of palaces of millionaires unroofed than to see desolation in the cabins of the poor.

Capital can do nothing without the assistance of labor. All there is of value in the world is the product of labor. Many employers have sought to balance their accounts by leaving something for universities, for the establishment of libraries, drinking fountains, or to build monuments to departed greatness. It would have been, I think, far better had they used this money to better the condition of the men who really earned it. I think the great railroads should pay pensions to their worn out employees. These great companies should take care of the men they maim. They should look out after the ones whose lives they have used and whose labor has been the foundation of their prosperity. It may be that the mechanics, the workingmen, will finally become intelligent enough to really unite, to act in absolute concert.

All men engaged in manufacturing are neither good nor generous. Many of them get work for as little as possible and sell its product for all they can get. It is impossible to adopt a policy that will not, by such people, be abused. Many of them would like to see the working man toil for twelve, fourteen, or sixteen hours in each day. Many of them wonder why they need sleep or food and are perfectly astonished when they ask for pay.

Let these men whom others have made wealthy give something to the workingman—something to those who created their fortunes. Do not let it be regarded as charity—let it be regarded as justice.

Capital has always claimed and still claims the right to combine. Manufacturers meet and determine upon prices in spite of the great law of supply and demand. Have the laborers the same right to counsel and combine? When the poor combine, it is "conspiracy". If they act in concert, if they really do something it is the "mob". Capital has the army and the navy, the legislative, the judicial and the executive departments.

How are we to settle the unequal contest between men and machines? Will the machine finally go into partnership with the laborer? Can these forces of nature be controlled for the benefit of her suffering children? Will extravagance keep pace with ingenuity? Will the workers become intelligent enough to be the owners of the machines? Will these giants, these titans, shorten or lengthen the hours of labor? Will they give leisure to the industrious or will they make the rich richer and the poor poorer?

Tenements and flats and rented lands are, in my judgement, the enemies of civilization. They make the rich richer and the poor poorer. They put a few in palaces but they put the many in prisons.

Men of great wealth, engaged in manufacturing, instead of giving $500,000 for a library, or a million dollars for a college, ought to put this money aside, invest it in bonds to the government, and the interest ought to be used in taking care of the old, of the helpless, of those who meet with accidents in their work. Under our laws if an employee is caught in a wheel or in a band,

and his arm or leg is torn off, he is left to the charity of the community, whereas the profits of business ought to support him in his old age. Now, it seems to me that a certain percent should be laid aside, so that every brakeman and conductor could feel that he was providing for himself, as well as for his fellow-workmen, so that when the dark days come there would be a little light.

Let every man teach his son, teach his daughter, that labor is honorable.

Lent

Lent is just as good as any other part of the year and no part can be too good to do good. It was not my object to hurt the feelings of Episcopalians and Catholics. If they think there is some subtle relation between hunger and heaven, or that faith depends upon or is strengthened by famine, or that veal during Lent is the enemy of virtue, or that beef breeds blasphemy while fish feeds faith, of course, all this is nothing to me. They have a right to say that vice depends on victuals, sanctity on soup, religion on rice and chastity on cheese, but they have no right to say that a lecture on Liberty is an insult to them because they are hungry.

Life

Is life worth living? Well, I can only answer for myself. I like to be alive, to breathe the air, to look at the landscape, the clouds, the stars, to repeat old poems, to look at pictures and statues, to hear music, the voices of the ones I love. I enjoy eating and smoking. I like good cold water. I like to talk with my wife, my girls, my grandchildren. I like to sleep and to dream. Yes, you can say that life, to me, is worth living.

When I was a boy I killed two ducks, and it hurt me as much as anything I ever did. No, I would not kill any living creature.

I want to live—I get great happiness out of life. I enjoy the company of my friends. I enjoy seeing the faces of the ones I love. I enjoy art and music. I love Shakespeare and Burns; love to hear the music of Wagner; love to see a good play. I take pleasure in eating and sleeping. The fact is, I like to breathe. I want to get all the happiness out of life that I can. I want to suck the orange dry, so that when death comes nothing but the peelings will be left. So, I say: "Long life!"

Love

Love is the only bow on Life's dark cloud. It is the morning and the evening star. It shines upon the babe, and sheds radiance on the quiet tomb. It is the mother of art, inspirer of poet, patriot and philosopher. It is the air and light of every heart—builder of every home, kindler of every fire on every hearth. It was the first to dream of immortality. It fills the world with melody—for music is the voice of love. Love is the magician, the enchanter, that changes worthless things to joy, and makes right royal kings and queens of common clay. It is the perfume of that wondrous flower, the heart, and without that sacred passion, that divine swoon, we are less than beasts; but with it, earth is heaven, and we are gods.

The greatest themes in poetry and song are love and death. In "Tristan and Isolde" is the greatest music of love and death. In Shakespeare the greatest themes are love and death. In all real poetry, in all real music, the dominant, the triumphant tone, is love . . . and the minor, the sad refrain, the shadow, the background, the mystery, is death.

It is a splendid thing to think that the woman you really love will never grow old to you. Through the wrinkles of time, through the masks of years, if you really love her, you will always see the face you loved and won. And a woman who really loves a man does not see that he grows old; he is not decrepit to her; he does not tremble; he is not old; she always sees the same gallant gentleman who won her hand and heart. I like to think that love is eternal. And to love in that way and then go down the hill of life together, and as you go down, hear, perhaps the laughter of grandchildren, while the birds of joy and love sing once more in the leafless branches of the tree of age.

The provincial prudes, and others of like mold, pretend that love is a duty rather than a passion—a kind of self-denial—not an overmastering joy. They preach the gospel of pretense and pantalettes. In the presence of sincerity, of truth, they cast down their eyes and endeavor to feel immodest. To them the most beautiful thing is hypocrisy adorned with a blush.

Marriage and Family

I believe in marriage, and I hold in utter contempt the opinions of those long haired men and short haired women who denounce the institution of marriage. I hold in the greater contempt the husband who would enslave his wife.

The real temple is the home; civilization rests upon the family.

Let me say right here, that I regard marriage as the holiest institution among men. Without the fireside there is no human advancement; without the family relation there is no life worth living. Every good government is made up of good families. The unit of good government is the family and anything that tends to destroy the family is perfectly devilish and infamous.

I believe in the fireside. I believe in the democracy of home. I believe in the republicanism of the family. I believe in liberty, equality and love.

The marriage of one man to the one woman is the citadel and fortress of civilization.

A few months ago, a priest made a confession—he could carry his secret no longer. He admitted that he was married—that he was a father of two children—that he had violated his priestly vows. He was unfrocked and cast out. After a time he came back and asked to be restored into the bosom of the church, giving as his reason that he had abandoned his wife and babes. This throws a flood of light on the theological view of marriage.

The indissoluble marriage was a reaction from polygamy.

Marriage is the most important contract that human beings can make.

Marriage to Eva Parker and Her Influence upon Ingersoll

The full influence of Eva upon Robert can never be adequately estimated. However, one thing is absolutely certain, Eva was everything, possessed every attribute that Robert required and wanted in a wife; every quality needed to help build, strengthen, enrich, and enoble his character and personality. She was the ballast for his sail, the compass on his ship of life. Robert Ingersoll enjoyed the incomparable blessing of a supremely happy home from the day of his marriage until the day of his death. For thirty eight years, husband and wife were intellectual and spiritual comrades as well as romantic lovers, sharing each other's beliefs, thoughts and emotions, consecrated to the same ideals and purposes. Robert inscribed his first published volume of lectures to, "My Wife, a Woman Without Superstition." (Eva Ingersoll Wakefield, granddaughter writing in 1951 in *The Letters of Robert Ingersoll.*)

Metaphysics

There is, however, no propriety in wasting any time about the science of metaphysics. I will give you my definition of metaphysics: Two fools get together; each admits what neither can prove, and thereupon both of them say, "hence we infer". That is all there is of metaphysics.

Mind (The)

The mind is a little piece of intellectual glass the surface of which is not true, not perfect. In consequence of this, every image is more or less distorted. The less we know, the more we imagine that we know; but the more we know, the smaller seems the sum of knowledge. The less we know, the more we expect, the more we hope for, and the more seems within the range of probability. The less we have the more we want. There never was a banquet magnificent enough to gratify the imagination of a begger. The moment that people begin to reason about what they call the supernatural, they seem to lose their minds.

The truth is, there can be no reply to the argument that man should be governed by his reason, that he should depend upon observation and experience. He should use the faculties he has for his own benefit and the benefit of his fellow-men. It is not within the power of man to substantiate the supernatural. It is beyond the power of evidence.

The human mind grows—and as it grows it abandons the old, and the old gets its revenge by maligning the new.

I have no doubt that the condition of the mind has some effect upon health. The blood, the heart, the lungs answer—respond—to emotion. There is no mind without body, and the body is affected by thought—by passion, by cheerfulness, by depression.

Still, I have not the slightest confidence in what is called "mind cure". I do not believe that thought, or any set of ideas, can cure a cancer, or prevent hair from falling out, or remove a tumor, or even freckles. Magic is not medicine.

Miracles

The real miracles are the facts in nature.

Believers in miracles should not endeavor to explain them. There is but one way to explain anything, and that is to account for it by natural agencies. The moment you explain a miracle, it disappears.

I want to see a good miracle. I want to see a man with one

leg, and then I want to see the other leg grow out. I would like to see a miracle like that performed in North Carolina. Two men were disputing about the relative merits of the salve they had for sale. One of the men, in order to demonstrate that his salve was better than any other, cut off a dog's tail and applied a little salve to the stump. In the presence of spectators, a new tail grew out. But the other man, who also had salve for sale, took up the piece of tail that had been cast away, put a little salve at the end of that, and a new dog grew out. The last heard of those parties, they were still quarrelling as to who owned the second dog. Something like that is what I call a miracle.

To do anything contrary to or without regard to the facts of nature is a miracle. We now believe that events have natural parents and that none die childless.

Ignorance is the soil in which belief in miracles grows.

. . . to do anything contrary to or without regard to the facts in nature is to perform a miracle.

Do away with the miracles, and the superhuman character of Christ is destroyed. He becomes what he really was—a man.

Inspiration is only necessary to give authority to that which is repugnant to human reason. Only that which never happened needs to be substantiated by miracles.

If we read in the annals of China that several thousand years ago, five thousand people were fed on one sandwich, and that several sandwiches were left over after the feast, there are few intelligent men (except, it may be, the editors of religious weeklies) who would credit the statement. But many intelligent people, reading a like story in the Hebrew, or in the Greek, or in a mistranslation from either of these languages, accept the story without a doubt.

Miscellany

A newspaper critic's review of an Ingersoll speech contained this declaration: "It could not boast neither of novelty in argument or of attractive language."

Ingersoll's response was characteristic. "After this, nothing should be noticed that this gentleman says on the subject of grammar."

The floods are still a terror, but in my judgement, the time will come when the floods will be controlled by the genius of man. The tributaries and the great rivers and their tributaries will be damned in such a way as to collect the waters of every flood and give them out gradually through all the year . . .

Niagara (Falls) fills the heavens with its song. Man will arrest the falling flood; he will change its force to electricity, that is to say, to light . . .

I have also heard it said that large sums of money will be withheld by certain old people who have the prospect of dying in the near future if the museums are open on Sunday.

There is not a man with genius enough, with brains enough to own five million dollars. Why? The money will own him. He becomes the key to a safe . . . We ought to teach our children that great wealth is a curse. Great wealth is the mother of crime.

In response to a question as to when he would resume his cross-country lecturing, Ingersoll replied: "I expect to after awhile. I am now waiting for the church to catch up. I got so far ahead that I began almost to sympathize with the clergy."

At the end of an extended interview, an eager young reporter asked: "Is there anything else bearing upon this question or that would make good reading that I have forgotten that you would like to say?"

Replied R.G.I.: "Yes, good-bye."

Thousands of errors have been propagated by honest men. As a rule mistakes get their wings from honest people. The testiιιιony of a witness to the happenings of the impossible gets no weight from the honesty of the witness.

Perhaps I have reached the age of discretion. But it may be that discretion is the enemy of happiness. If the buds had discretion there might be no fruit. So it may be that the follies committed in the spring give autumn the harvest.

Very few people have the opportunity of selecting their own parents, and it is exceedingly difficult in the matter of grandparents.

The only objection I have to horse racing is its cruelty. The whip and the spur should be banished from the track. Abolish torture on the track and let the best horse win.

For thirty years Edmund Burke was known in Parliament as the "Dinner Bell"—whenever he rose to speak, everybody went to dinner.

Negroes (Blacks) (see also Civil Rights)

We hesitated to allow the Negro to fight for his own freedom—hesitated to let him wear the uniform of the nation while he battled for the supremacy of its flag.

It is very easy to see why the colored people should hate us, but why we should hate them is beyond my comprehension. They never sold our wives. They never robbed our cradles. They never scarred our backs. They never pursued us with bloodhounds. They never branded our flesh.

The colored people do not ask for revenge—they simply ask for justice.

Above all things—educate your children . . . Nothing gives me more pleasure than to see your little children with books under their arms, going and coming from school . . . But it is not for me to give you advice. Your conduct has been above all praise. You have been as patient as the earth beneath, as the stars above. You have been law abiding and industrious. You have not offensively asserted your rights, or offensively borne your wrongs. You have returned good for evil. When I remember that the ancestors of my race were in universities and colleges and common schools while you and your fathers were on the auction-block, in the slave-pen, or in the field beneath the cruel lash, in states where reading and writing were crimes, I am astonished at the progress you have made.

Editor's Note: In a letter to Ingersoll, Paul Lawrence Dunbar (1872-1906) credited Ingersoll with being the "key that opened the door to a job in the Library in Washington, D.C."

Oaths/Oathtaking

The objection to the oath is this: It furnishes a falsehood with a letter of credit . . . The oath is a mask that falsehood puts on, and for a moment is mistaken for truth. It gives to dishonesty the advantage of solemnity.

I think it would be a thousand times better to abolish all oaths in courts of justice. The oath allows the rascal to put on the garments of solemnity, the mask of piety, while he tells a lie.

Orthodox Clergy, Missionaries, Revivalists

From the papers I see that they (the clergy) are busy trying to find out who the wife of Cain was. I see that the Rev. Dr. Robinson of New York is now wrestling with that problem. He begins to doubt as to whether Adam was the first man, whether Eve was the first woman. He suspects there were other races, and that Cain did not marry his sister, but somebody else's sister, and that somebody else was not Cain's brother. One can hardly over-estimate the importance of these questions, they have such a direct bearing on the progress of the world. If it should turn out that Adam was the first man, or that he was not the first man, something might happen—I am not prepared to say what, but it might. It is a curious kind of spectacle to see a few hundred people paying a few thousand dollars a year for the purpose of having these great problems discussed: "Was Adam the first man? Who was Cain's wife? Has anyone seen a map of the land of Nod? Where are the four rivers than ran murmuring through the groves of Paradise? Who was the snake? How did he walk? What language did he speak?" This turns a church into a kind ot nursery, makes a cradle of each pew, and gives to each member a rattle with which he can amuse what he calls his mind. The great theologians of Andover have been disputing among themselves as to what is to become of the heathen who fortunately died before meeting any missionary from that institution. One can almost afford to be damned hereafter for the sake of avoiding the dogmas of Andover here.

Every minister likes to consider himself as a brave shepherd leading the lambs through green pastures and defending them at night from Infidel wolves. All this he does for a certain share of the wool.

I am not trying to destroy another world. I am trying to prevent the theologians from destroying this world.

The clergy know, I know, that they know that they do not know.

Of all the failures of which we have any history or knowledge, the missionary effort is the most conspicuous. The whole question has been decided here, in our own country, and conclusively settled. We have nearly exterminated the Indians, but we have converted none.

If the ministers had their way, there would be no form of human enjoyment except prayer, signing subscription papers, putting money in contribution boxes, listening to sermons, reading the cheerful histories of the Old Testament, imagining the joys of heaven and the torments of hell. The church is opposed to the theater, is the enemy of the opera, looks upon dancing as a crime, hates billiards, despises cards, opposes roller-skating, and even entertains a certain prejudice against croquet.

Men give millions of dollars to carry the gospel to the heathen, and leave their own neighbors without bread. These same people insist on closing libraries and museums of art on Sunday, and yet Sunday is the only day that these institutions can be visited by the poor. They even want to stop the street cars so that these workers, these men and women, cannot go to the parks or the fields on Sunday. They want stages stopped on fashionable avenues so that the rich may not be disturbed in their prayers and devotions.

I regard these revivals as essentially barbaric. The fire that has to be blown all the time is a poor thing to get warm by. I think they do no good but much harm; they make innocent people think they are guilty, and the very mean people think they are good . . . I think that neither men nor women should be engaged in frightening people into heaven. That is all I wish to say on the subject, as I do not think it worth talking about.

The Rev. Mr. Munger has suddenly become a revivalist. According to the papers he is sought in every direction. His popularity seems to rest on the fact that he brutally beat a girl twelve years old because she did not say her prayers to suit him. Muscular Christianity is what the ignorant people want.

Orthodox Religions

Belief without evidence is not religion; faith without facts is not religion.

I have no confidence in any religion that can be demonstrated only to children. I suspect all creeds that rely implicitly on mothers and nurses.

My belief is that the supernatural has had its day. The church must change or abdicate. That is to say, it must keep step with the progress of the world or be trampled under foot. The church must keep up with the people. The multitude care little about controversies in churches; they do care about the practical questions that affect their daily lives.

A church that preaches the eternity of punishment has within it the seed of all barbarism and the soil to make it grow.

I have little confidence in any enterprise or business or investment that promises dividends only after the death of the stockholders.

The church sells crime on credit.

Every church cries: "Believe and give".

Supernatural religion will fade from the world; in its place we shall have reason.

In the dear old religious days the earth was flat—a little dishing, if anything—and just above it was Jehovah's house, and just below was where the Devil lived. God and his angels inhabited the third floor, the Devil and his imps the basement, and the human race the second floor.

When the theologian governed the world, it was covered with huts and hovels for the many, palaces and cathedrals for the few. To nearly all the children of men, reading and writing were unknown arts. The day of Science dawned, and the luxuries of a century ago are the necessities of today.

Casting out devils was a certificate of divinity.

All religions, so far as I know, claim to have been miraculously founded, miraculously preserved, and miraculously propagated. The priests of all claimed to have messages from God, and claimed to have a certain authority, and the miraculous has always been appealed to for the purpose of substantiating the message and the authority.

Every church that has a standard higher than human welfare is dangerous.

Beyond the region of the Probable is the Possible, and beyond the Possible is the Impossible and beyond the Impossible are the religions of this world.

Any man who believes that he can make some God happy, by making himself miserable is superstitious. Anyone who believes he can gain happiness in another world by raising hell with his fellow man in this, is simply superstitious. . . . he who believes that there is, or that there can be any other religious duty than to increase the happiness of mankind in the world now and here, is simply superstitious.

Religion tries to force all minds into one mould. Knowing that all cannot believe, the church endeavors to make all say they believe. She longs for the unity of hypocrisy . . .

Who can imagine the infinite impudence of a church assuming to think for the human race?

I want it distinctly understood . . . that while I am opposed to Catholicism I am not opposed to Catholics—while I am opposed to Presbyterianism I am not opposed to Presbyterians. I do not fight people, I fight ideas, I fight principles, and I never go into personalities . . . I attack certain principles because I think they are wrong, but I always want it understood that I have nothing against persons—nothing against victims.

Catholics and Protestants

The Catholics have a Pope. Protestants laugh at them, and yet the Pope is capable of intellectual advancement. In addition to this, the Pope is mortal, and the church cannot be afflicted with the same idiot forever. The Protestants have a book for their Pope. The book cannot advance. Year after year, and century after century, the book remains as ignorant as ever.

Other Lands, Other People

China and the Chinese

If we wish to prevent the immigration of the Chinese, let us reform our treaties with the vast empire from whence they came. For thousands of years the Chinese secluded themselves from the rest of the world. . . . . We forced ourselves upon them. We called, not with cards but with cannon. The English battered down the door in the names of opium and Christ. This infamy was regarded as another triumph for the gospel. At last, in self-defense, the Chinese allowed Christians to touch their shores. Their wise men, their philosophers protested and prophesied that time would show that Christians could not be trusted. This report proves that the wise men were not only philosophers but prophets. Treat China as you would England. Keep a treaty while it is in force.

At first a demand was made that the Chinese should be driven out, then that no others should be allowed to come and laws with these objects in view were passed, in spite of the treaties preventing the coming of any more. For a time that satisfied the haters of the Mongolian. Then came a demand for more stringent legislation so that many of the Chinese already here could be compelled to leave.

Cuba (February 1898)

I want Cuba to be free. I want Spain driven from the Western World. She has already starved five hundred thousand Cubans—poor helpless noncombatants . . . This country ought to stop this gigantic crime. We should do this in the name of humanity—for the sake of the starving, the dying.

I want Cuba whenever Cuba wants us, and I favor the idea of getting her in the notion of wanting us. I want it in the interest, as I believe, of humanity, of progress; in other words of human liberty. That is what the war was waged for . . . They fought in the first righteous war; I mean righteous in the sense that we fought for the liberty of others.

I believe that Cuba is to be free, and I want that island to give a new flag to the air, whether it ever becomes a part of the U.S. or not. My sympathies are all with those who are struggling for their rights, trying to get the clutch of tyranny from their throats.

Hawaiian Islands

I would like to see the Sandwich Islands annexed to the U.S. They are a good way from San Francisco and our western shore, but they are nearer to us than they are to any other nation. I think they would be of great importance. They would tend to increase the Asiatic trade, and they certainly would be important in case of war. We should have fortifications on those islands that no naval power could take.

Ireland

I believe in liberty for Ireland, not because it is Ireland, but because they are human beings, and I am for liberty, not as a prejudice but as a principle . . . Ireland should govern herself . . . The treatment of Ireland by England has been one continuous crime. There is no meaner page in history.

I do not think that we have any interest in the dispute between Venezuela and England. It was and is none of our business. The Monroe Doctrine was not and is not in any way involved. Mr. Cleveland made a mistake and so did Congress.

Mexican War

. . . we had a war with Mexico, in which we got a good deal of glory and one million square miles of land, but little honor. I will admit that we got but little honor out of that war. That territory they wanted to give to the slaveholder.

Philippine Islands

I want the Philippines if the Filipinos want us. I do not want to conquer and enslave those people. The war on the Filipinos is a great mistake—a blunder—almost a crime . . . We had no right to buy, because Spain had no right to sell the Philippines. We acquired no rights on those islands by whipping Spain.

Russia (1884)

How do you account for Russia? How do you account for Siberia? How do you account for the fact that whole races of men toiled beneath the master's lash for ages without recompense and without reward? What evidence can you find that this universe is presided over by an infinitely wise and good God?

In a country like Russia, where every mouth is a bastile and every tongue a convict, there may be some excuse to be a Nihilist. Where the noblest and the best are driven to Siberia, there may be a reason for the Nihilist.

A Nihilist may be forgiven in Russia—may even be praised in Russia. (1886)

I have said frequently that if I lived in Russia I should in all probability be a Nihilist. I can conceive of no government that would not be as good as that of Russia, and I would consider NO government far preferable to that government. Any possible state of anarchy is better than organized crime, because in the chaos of anarchy justice may be done by accident. In a government organized for the perpetuation of slavery, and for the purpose of crushing out of the human brain every noble thought, justice does not live.

Peace and War

War destroys. Peace creates. War is decay and death. Peace is growth and life—sunlight and air. War kills men. Peace maintains them. Artillery does not reason; it asserts. A bayonet has point enough, but no logic. When the sword is drawn, reason remains in the scabbard.

Editor's Note: The reader should not assume on the basis of this quote that Ingersoll was a pacifist. Far from it, there are hundreds of pages devoted to extolling the heroic exploits of his comrades in the Civil War.

Politics/Politicians

I would also like to liberate the politicians. At present, the successful office-seeker is a good deal like the center of the earth, he weighs nothing himself, but draws everything else to him. There are so many societies, so many churches, so many isms, that it is almost impossible for an independent man to succeed in a political career. Candidates are forced to pretend that they are Catholics with Protestant proclivities, or Christians with liberal tendencies, or temperance men who now and then take a glass of wine, or, that although not members of any church their wives are, and that they subscribe liberally to all. The result of all this is that we reward hypocrisy and elect men entirely destitute to real principle. This will never change until the people become grand enough to allow each other to do their own thinking.

Legislators are, for the most part, controlled by those who, by their wealth and influence, elect them. The few, in reality, cast the votes of the many, and the few influence the ones voted for by the many. Special interests being active, secure special legislation, and the object of special legislation is to create a kind of monopoly—that is to say, to get some advantage. Chiefs, barons, priests, and kings ruled, robbed, destroyed and duped, and their places have been taken by corporations, monopolists, and politicians. The large fish still live on the little ones, and the fine theories have, as yet, failed to change the condition of mankind.

In this country, where the divorce has been granted between church and state, the religious opinions of candidates should be let alone. To make inquiry is a piece of impertinence—a piece of impudence. I have voted for men of all persuasions and expect to keep right on. If they are not civilized enough to give me the liberty they ask for themselves, why I shall simply set an example of decency.

I object to no man who is running for office on the ticket of my party on account of his religious convictions. I care nothing

about the church of which he is a member. That is his business.
That is an individual matter—something with which the State
has no right to interfere—something with which no party can
rightfully have anything to do.

In my opinion, both parties will nail anti-trust planks in
their platform. But this talk is a lot of bosh with both parties.
Neither one is honest in its cry against the trusts. The one making the more noise in this direction may get the votes of some
unthinking persons, but everyone who is capable of reading and digesting what he reads, knows full well that the leaders
of neither party are sincere and honest in their demonstrations
against trusts.

People are thoroughly disgusted with machine politics, and
demand politics without any machine.

Tammany Hall bears the same relation to the penitentiary
that the Sunday School does to the church.

There are two kinds of people that I have no use
for—leaders and followers. The leader should be principle; the
leader should be a great object to be accomplished. The fol-
lower should be the man dedicated to the accomplishment of a
noble end.

I believe in joining the party that is going nearest your way.
I do not believe in being the slave or serf or servant of a party.
Go with it if it is going your road, and when the road forks, take
the one that leads to the place you want to visit, no matter
whether the party goes that way or not. I do not believe in belonging to a party or being the property of any organization. I
do not believe in giving a mortgage on yourself, or a deed of
trust for any purpose whatsoever. It is better to be free and vote
wrong than to be a slave and vote right. I believe in taking the
chances. At the same time, as long as the party is going my way,
I believe in placing that party above particular persons, and if
that party nominates a man that I despise, I will vote for him if
he is going my way. I would rather have a bad man belonging to

my party in place, than a good man belonging to the other, provided my man believes in my principles, and to that extent I believe in party loyalty.

I do not belong to the Republican party, but I have been going with it, and when it goes wrong I shall quit, unless the other is worse. There is no office, no place, that I want, and as it does not cost anything to be right, I think it better to be that way.

I do not believe President Hayes dare appoint me U.S. Minister to Germany. He is afraid of the religious world.

"Col., what are the glaring mistakes of Cleveland's administration?" First, accepting the nomination. Second, taking the oath of office. Third, not resigning.

Ingersoll's response to possible nomination for Republican Party ticket for Governor of Illinois: Gentleman, I am not asking to be governor of Illinois. I have in my composition that which I have declared to the world as my views upon religion. My position I would not, under any circumstances, not even for my life, seem to renounce. I would rather refuse to be President of the United States than to do so. My religious belief is my own. It belongs to me, not to the State of Illinois. I would not smother one sentiment of my heart to be the emperor of the round globe.
Editor's Note: The nomination was given to somebody else! (1868)

Polygamy and the Mormons

I hate the system of polygamy. Nothing is more infamous. I admit the Old Testament upholds it. I admit that the patriarchs were mostly polygamists. I admit that Solomon was mistaken on that subject . . . At the same time if you undertake to get that idea out of the Mormons by force you will not succeed . . . I do not believe in the bayonet plan. Mormonism must be done away with by the thousand influences of civilization, by education, by the elevation of the people. Of course, a gentleman would rather have one noble woman than a hundred females.

Poverty

Most of the intellectual giants of the world have been nursed at the breast of poverty.

Granaries bursting and famine looking into the doors of the poor! Millions of everything, and yet millions wanting everything and having substantially nothing! Now, there is something wrong here. My sympathies are with the poor. My sympathies are with the workingmen of the U.S. . . . . I do not believe in the tyranny of government, but I do believe in justice as between man and man.

My heart beats with those who bear the burdens of this poor world.

Commenting on the platform of Henry George who was running for mayor of New York City at the time (1886): I do not understand that George is a Socialist. He is on the side of those who work—so am I. He wants to help those that work—so do I. He wants to help those that need help—so do I. The rich can take care of themselves. I shed no tears over the miseries of capital. I think of the men in mines, factories, in huts, hovels, and cellars, of the poor sewing women, of the poor, hungry, and despairing. The world must be made better through intelligence. I do not go with the destroyers, with those who hate the successful, that hate the generous simply because they are rich. Wealth is the surplus produced by labor, and the wealth of the world should keep the world from want . . . It is very probable that all of us will be dead before all of the theories of Mr. George are put in practice. Some of them, however, may at some time benefit mankind; and as far as I am concerned, I am willing to hasten the day, although it may not come while I live.

How a human being can consent to live on profit from poverty, is beyond my imagination.

There must be some way for the rich and the poor to get acquainted.

If nobody has too much everybody will have enough. Wealth is not a crime and poverty is not a virtue—although the virtuous have generally been poor.

Prayer/Praying

The last Scientific Congress in America was opened with a prayer. Think of a science that depends on the efficacy of words addressed to the Unknown and Unknowable.

"Never will I seek or receive private or individual salvation. Never will I enter into final bliss alone. But forever and everywhere will I labor and strive for the final redemption of every creature throughout all worlds, until all are redeemed. Never will I wrongly leave this world to sin, sorrow and struggle, but will remain and work and suffer where I am." This is the prayer of the Brahmins, a prayer that has trembled from human lips toward heaven for more than four thousand years. Has the orthodox religion produced a prayer like this?

All the prayer in the world cannot take the place of the circulation of the blood. All the prayer in the world is no substitute for digestion. All the prayer in the world cannot take the place of food; and whenever a man lives by prayer, you will find that he eats considerable besides.

I have no objection to anybody's praying. Those who think that prayers are answered should pray. For all who honestly believe this, and who honestly implore their Deity to watch over, protect, and save the life of the President, I have only the kindest feelings . . . Personally, I have not the slightest idea of the existence of the supernatural. Prayer may affect the person who prays. It may put him in such a frame of mind that he can better bear disappointment than if he had not prayed; but I cannot believe that there is any being who hears and answers prayer.

. . . all prayers die in the air which they uselessly agitate.

Think of the egotism of a man who believes that an infinite being wants his praise!

The man who invented the telescope found out more about heaven than the closed eyes of prayer ever discovered.

The assassin cannot sanctify his dagger by falling on his knees, and it does not help a falsehood if it be uttered as a prayer. Religion, used to intensify the hatred of men toward men under the pretense of pleasing God, has cursed this world.

Years ago I took the ground that shutting the eyes in prayer is a souvenir of sun worship. People who addressed the sun had to close their eyes and afterwards, when they worshipped images adorned with jewels, they pretended that their faces were so bright that they could not look upon them. So it was a kind of flattery to close the eyes, and this habit was persisted in, although no one now pretends to see the God, or object worshipped.

One time while staying at a hotel at Virginia Beach, a wind of hurricane proportions came up during the night. The noise and clatter was terrific. Most of the patrons gathered in the hotel lobby and started to pray. Their vigil was interrupted by the Col., descending the stairs clad in nightshirt and slippers. An anxious member of the prayer circle inquired, "Are you going to join us in prayer?"
"No, I came down to see if breakfast was ready!"

To plow is to pray; to plant is to prophesy.

The hands that help are better far than the lips that pray.

Press/Newspapers

... the Press should appeal only to the highest and to the noblest in the human heart ... Let the Press have the courage always to defend the right, always to defend the people—and let it always have the power to clutch and strangle any combination of men, however intellectual or cunning or rich that feeds and fattens on the flesh of honest men.

I have just one little fault to find with the tendency of the modern press to go into personal affairs—into so-called private affairs. I am not so much opposed to what is called sensationalism, for that must exist as long as crime is considered news, and believe me, when virtue becomes news it can only be when this will have become an exceedingly bad world. At the same time, I think that the publication of crime may have more or less the tendency of increasing it.

The editor or manager of a newspaper occupies a public position, and he must not treat his patrons as though they were weak and ignorant children. He must not, in the interest of any ism, suppress the truth—neither must he be dictated to by any church or any society of believers or unbelievers. The Telegram by its course, has given a certificate of its manliness, and the public by its course, has certified that it appreciates true courage.

Every article in a newspaper should be signed by the writer. And all the writers should do their best to tell the exact facts.

Prohibition and Temperance

In response to the agitation for an Amendment to the Constitution for Prohibition, R.G.I. observed: The people of this country, no matter how much they may deplore the evils of intemperance, are not yet willing to set on foot a system of spying into each other's affairs. They know that prohibition would need thousands of officers—that it would breed informers and spies and peekers and skulkers by the hundred in every country. They know that laws do not of themselves make good people. Good people make good laws . . . Americans do not wish to be temperate upon compulsion.

I am opposed to prohibition and always have been, and hope always to be. I do not want the Legislature to interfere in these matters. I do not believe that the people can be made temperate by law.

You never can make great men and great women by keeping them out of the way of temptation. You have to educate them to withstand temptation. It is all nonsense to tie a man's hands behind him and then praise him for not picking pockets. I believe that temperance walks hand in hand with liberty.

All men should be temperate.

The best temperance lecture in the fewest words, you will find in Victor Hugo's great novel, "Les Miserables". The grave digger is asked to take a drink. He refuses and gives this reason: "The hunger of my family is the enemy of my thirst."

Drunkenness is one form of intemperance, prohibition is another . . .

Take wine and malt liquors out of the world and we shall lose a great deal of good fellowship. The world would lose more than it would gain. There is a certain sociability about wine that I should hate to have taken from the earth. Strong liquors the folks had better let alone. If prohibition succeeds, and wines and malt liquors go, the next thing will be to take tobacco away, and the next thing all other pleasures until prayer meetings will be the only places of enjoyment.

Physicians become popular in proportion as liquor of some kind figures in their prescriptions. Then in the towns, clubs are formed—the principal object being to establish a saloon, and in many instances the drug store becomes a favorite resort, especially on Sundays. There is, however, another side to this question. It is this: Nothing in this world is more important than personal liberty. Many people are in favor of blotting out the sun to prevent the growth of weeds. This is the mistake of all prohibitory fanaticism.

Property

No man should be allowed to own any land that he does not use.
Everybody knows that—I do not care whether he has thousands
or millions. I have owned a great deal of land, but I know just as
well as I know I am living that I should not be allowed to have it
unless I use it. And why? Don't you know that if people could
bottle the air, they would? Don't you know there would be an
American Air-bottling Association? And don't you know that
they would allow thousands and millions to die for want of
breath, if they could not pay for the air? . . . Now, the land belongs to the children of Nature. . . . It seems to me that every
child of Nature is entitled to his share of the land . . . he should
not be compelled to beg the privilege to work the soil, of a babe
that happened to be born before him. . . . it is not in our interest
to have a few landlords and millions of tenants.

Real Bible (The)

For thousands of years men have been writing the real Bible,
and it is being written from day to day, and it will never be
finished while man has life. All the facts that we know, all the
truly recorded events, all the discoveries and inventions, all the
wonderful machines whose wheels and levers seem to think, all
the poems, crystals from the brain, flowers from the heart, all
the songs of love and joy, of smiles and tears, the great dramas
of Imagination's world, the wondrous paintings, miracles of
form and color, of light and shade, the marvelous marbles that
seem to live and breathe, the secrets told by rock and star, by
dust and flower, by rain and snow, by frost and flame, by winding stream and desert sand, by mountain range and billowed
sea.

All the wisdom that lengthens and enobles life—all that
avoids or cures disease, or conquers pain—all just and perfect
laws and rules that guide and shape our lives, all thoughts that
feed the flames of love, the music that transfigures, enraptures
and enthralls, the victories of heart and brain, the miracles that
hands have wrought, the deft and cunning hands of those who
worked for wife and child, the histories of noble deeds, of brave

and useful men, of faithful loving wives, of quenchless mother love, of conflicts for the right, of sufferings for the truth, of all the best that all the men and women of the world have said, and thought and done through all the years.

These treasures of the heart and brain—these are the Sacred Scriptures of the human race.

Religion of Humanity

I am not a materialist, because I do not know what matter is. I am simply a naturalist—believe what I have to believe, what my senses certify is true, and my reason, after cross-examining the senses, approves. (Letters)

Let us live for man. Let us remember that those who have sought for the truths of nature have never persecuted their fellow-men. The astronomers and chemists have forged no chains, built no dungeons. The geologists have invented no instruments of torture. The philosophers have not demonstrated the truth of their theories by burning their neighbors. The great infidels, the thinkers, have lived for the good of man.

I believe in turning our attention to things of importance—to questions that may by some possibility be solved. It is of no importance to me whether God exists or not. I exist, and it is important to me to be happy while I exist. Therefore, I had better turn my attention to finding out the secret of happiness, instead of trying to ascertain the secret of the universe.

We are laying the foundations of the grand temple of the future—not the temple of all the gods, but of all the people—wherein with appropriate rites, will be celebrated the religion of Humanity. We are doing what little we can to hasten the coming of the day when society shall cease producing millionaires and mendicants—gorged indolence and famished industry.

Humanity is the grand religion, and no God can put a man in hell in another world, who has made a little heaven in this.

God cannot make a man miserable if that man had made some-body else happy. God cannot hate anybody who is capable of loving anybody. Humanity—that word embraces all there is.

Col., will the religion of humanity be the religion of the future? "Yes; it is the only religion now. All other is superstition. Humanity is the only possible religion."

If abuses are destroyed, man must destroy them. If slaves are freed, man must free them. If new truths are discovered, man must discover them. If the naked are clothed; if the hungry are fed; if justice is done; if labor is rewarded; if superstition is driven from the mind; if the defenseless are protected and if the right finally triumphs, all must be the work of man. The grand victories of the future must be won by man, and by man alone.

Man must learn to rely upon himself. Reading bibles will not protect him from the blasts of winter, but houses, fire and clothing will. To prevent famine one plow is worth a million ser-mons and even patent medicines will cure more diseases than all the prayers uttered since the world began.

I prefer to make no being responsible. I prefer to say: If the naked are clothed, man must clothe them; if the hungry are fed, man must feed them. I prefer to rely on human endeavor, upon human intelligence, upon the heart and brain of man. There is no evidence that God ever interfered in the affairs of man. The hand of earth is stretched uselessly towards heaven. From the clouds there comes no help. In vain the shipwrecked cry to God. In vain the imprisoned ask for liberty and light—the world moves on, and the heavens are deaf, dumb, and blind. The frost freezes, the fire burns, slander smites, the wrong triumphs, the good suffer, and prayer dies upon the lips of faith.

Religion is like a palm tree—it grows at the top. The dead leaves are all orthodox, while the new ones are all heretics.

The first great step toward national reformation is the uni-versal acceptance of the idea that there is no escape from the consequences of our acts. . . . I cannot believe that moral character will be weakened by the statement that there is no escape from the consequences of our acts.

If there is a man in the world who is not willing to give to every human being every right he claims for himself, he is just so much nearer a barbarian than I am. It is a question of honesty. The man who is not willing to give to every other the same intellectual rights he claims for himself, is dishonest, selfish and brutal.

When the rights of even one human being are held in contempt the rights of all are in danger. We cannot destroy the liberties of others without losing our own. By exciting the prejudices of the ignorant we at last produce a contempt for law and justice, and sow the seeds of violence and crime.

We are under no obligation to stand still and allow ourselves to be murdered by one who honestly thinks that it is his duty to take our lives.

Come, wear your hair as you please. I say, Liberty to all. If I want to go to church, I'll go. If I want to hear a Calvinist preach, I will go—but I don't think I'll go this year. Let everybody do what he wants to. It won't be long until the joss house will be built by the side of the churches.

. . . Let us judge each other by our actions, not by theories. Not by what we happen to believe—because that depends very much on where we were born.

I believe in helping people to help themselves. I believe that corporations, and successful men, and superior men intellectually, should do all within their power to keep from robbing their fellowmen. The superior man should protect the inferior. The powerful should be the shield of the weak. Today, it is, for the most part, exactly the other way. The failures among men become the food of success.

Rouse yourself to do all useful things, to reach with thought and deed the ideal in your brain, to give your fancies wing, that they, like chemist bees, may find art's nectar in the weeds of common things, to look with trained and steady eyes for facts, to find the subtle threads that join the distant with the now, to increase knowledge, to take burdens from the weak, to develop the brain, to defend the right, to make a place for the soul. This is real religion. This is real worship.

The man who would sacrifice the well-being of man to please an imaginary phantom that he calls God is also dangerous. The only safe standard is the well-being of man in this world. Whenever this world is sacrificed for the sake of another, a mistake has been made. The only God that man can know is the aggregate of all beings capable of suffering and joy within the reach of his influence. To increase the happiness of such beings is to worship the only God man can know.

I do believe in the nobility of human nature. I believe in love and home, kindness and humanity. I believe in good fellowship and cheerfulness, in making wife and children happy. I believe in good nature, in giving to others all of the rights that you claim for yourself. I believe in free thought, in reason, observation, and experience. I believe in self-reliance and in expressing your honest thought. I have hope for the whole human race. What will happen to one will, I hope, happen to all and that, I hope, will be good. Above all, I believe in liberty.

True religion is not a theory—it is a practice. It is not a creed—it is a life. True religion is subordination of the passions to the perceptions of the intellect.

Religion has not civilized man—man has civilized religion.

Religion does not consist in worshipping gods, but in aiding the well-being, the happiness of man. No human being knows whether any god exists or not. All that has been said and written about "our god" or the gods of other people has no known fact or foundation. Words without thoughts, clouds without rain. Let us put theology out of religion.

Religion and morality have nothing in common, and yet there is no religion except the practice of morality. What you call religion is simply superstition.

Real religion means the doing of justice. Real religion means the giving to others every right you claim yourself. Real religion consists in duties of man to man, in feeding the hungry, in clothing the naked, in defending the innocent, and in saying what you believe to be true.

A religion that does not command the respect of the greatest minds will, in a little while, excite the mockery of all.

I am a believer in the home. . . I believe that the home, the family, is the unit of good government. . . That is all there is in this world worth living for. Honor, place, fame, glory, riches—they are ashes, smoke, dust, disappointment, unless there is somebody in the world you love, somebody who loves you; unless there is someplace where you can feel the arms of children around your neck, some place that is made absolutely sacred by the love of others.

I say, religion is all here in this world—right here—and that all our duties are right here to our fellowmen; that the man who builds a home, marries the girl that he loves, takes good care of her, likes the family, stays home nights, as a general thing; pays his debts, tries to find out what he can, gets all the ideas and beautiful things that his mind will hold, turns a part of his brain into a gallery of fine arts, has a host of paintings and statues there, then has another niche devoted to music—a magnificent dome, filled with winged notes that rise to glory—now, the man who does that gets all he can from the great ones dead; swaps all the thoughts he can with those alive, true to the ideal that he has here in his brain—he is what I call a religious man, because he makes the world better and happier. He puts the dimples of joy in the cheeks of the ones he loves, and he lets the gods run heaven to suit themselves.

Astrology was displaced by astronomy. Alchemy and black art gave way to chemistry. Science is destined to take the place of religion. In my judgement, the religion of the future will be Reason.

We need the religion of the real, the faith that rests on fact. Let us turn our attention to this world—the world in which we live.

I believe in the religion of the body—of physical development.

I will not sacrifice the world I have for one I know not of. I will not live here in fear, when I do not know that that which I fear lives. I am going to live a perfectly free man. I am going to reap the harvest of my mind, no matter how poor it is. . .

I insist, happiness is the end—virtue the means—and anything that wipes a tear from the face of man is good.

The only authority is Nature—the facts we know.

I do believe in the religion of justice, of kindness. I believe in humanity. I do believe that usefulness is the highest possible form of worship. The useful man is the good man; the useful man is the real saint. I care nothing about supernatural myths and mysteries, but I do care for human beings.

Real love and real religion are in no danger from science.

Do right, not to deny yourself but because you love yourself and because you love others.

A good deed is the best prayer; a loving life is the best religion.

I would not kill any living creature. I am sometimes tempted to kill a mosquito on my hand, but I stop to think what a wonderful construction it has, and shoo it away.

I have no reverence for a falsehood.

Nothing can be more sacred than a home, no altar purer than the hearth.

"Col., if you should write your last sentence on religious topics what would be your closing?" I now, in the presence of death affirm and reaffirm the truth of all that I have said against the superstitions of the world.

My creed is this: Happiness is the only good. The place to be happy is here. The time to be happy is now. The way to be happy is to make others so.

My doctrine is this: All true religion is embraced in the word Humanity. (Letters)

Salvation

We are told, however, that a way has been provided for the salvation of all men, and that in this plan the infinite mercy of God is made manifest to the children of men. According to the great scheme of atonement, the innocent suffers for the guilty in order to satisfy a law. What kind of law must it be that is satisfied with the agony of innocence? Who made this law? If God made it he must have known that the innocent would have to suffer as a consequence. The whole scheme is to me a melody of contradictions, impossibilities and theological conclusions. We are told that if Adam and Eve had not sinned in the Garden of Eden death never would have entered the world. We are further informed that had it not been for the devil, Adam and Eve would not have been led astray; and if they had not, as I said before, death never would have touched with its icy hand the human heart. If our first parents had never sinned, and death never had entered the world, you and I never would have existed. The earth would have been filled thousands of generations before you and I were born. At the feast of life, death made seats vacant for us. If there had been no sin—no death. If there had been no death the world would have been filled ages before you and I were born.

So far as I am concerned, I fail to see any mercy in the plan of salvation. Is it mercy to reward a man forever in consideration of believing a certain thing, the truth of which there is, to his mind, ample testimony? Is it mercy to punish a man with eternal fire simply because there is not testimony enough to satisfy his mind? Can there be such a thing as mercy in eternal punishment?

And yet this same Deity says to me, "resist not evil; pray for those that despitefully use you; love your enemies, but I will eternally damn mine." It seems to me that even gods should practice what they preach.

All atonement, after all is a kind of moral bankruptcy. Under its provisions man is allowed the luxury of sinning upon a credit. Whenever he is guilty of a wicked action he says, "Charge it". This kind of bookkeeping, in my judgement, tends to breed extravagance in sin. The truth is, most Christians are better than their creeds; most creeds are better than the Bible, and most men are better than their God.

Neither do I believe that thought is dangerous. It is incredible that only idiots are absolutely sure of salvation. It is incredible that the more brain you have the less your chance is. There can be no danger in honest thought.

Science and Nature

The religions of today are the sciences of the past. It may be that the sciences of today will be the religions of the future, and the other sciences will be as far beyond them as the science of today is beyond the religion of today. As a rule religion is a sanctified mistake and heresy a slandered fact.

Science holds with honest hand the scales wherein are weighed the facts and the fictions of the world.

In nature everything lives on something else. Life feeds upon life.

The sciences are not sectarian. Science is for this world, for the use of man.

Morality and religion must find their foundations in the necessary nature of things.

... in nature there are neither rewards nor punishments—there are consequences.

The universe is natural.

About this world little is known—about another world, nothing.

Nature is but an endless series of efficient causes. She cannot create but she eternally transforms. There is no beginning and there can be no end.

The sciences are not bound by the creeds. We should remember that there are no such things as Methodist mathematics, or Baptist botany, or Catholic chemistry. The sciences are secular.

I am perfectly satisfied that there is, and can be, no force without matter; that everything that is—all phenomena—all actions and thoughts, all exhibitions of force have a material basis—that nothing exists, ever did, or ever will exist, apart from matter. So I am satisfied that no matter ever existed, or ever will, apart from force.

The church never wanted disease to be under the control of man. Timothy Dwight, President of Yale College, preached a sermon against vaccination. His idea was that if God had decreed from all eternity that a certain man should die with the smallpox, it was a frightful sin to avoid and annul that decree by the trick of vaccination. Smallpox being regarded as one of the heaviest guns in the arsenal of heaven, to spike it was the height of presumption.

As vivisection is generally practiced it is an unspeakable cruelty . . . If these vivisectionists would give chloroform or ether to the animals they dissect; if they would render them insensible to pain, and if, by cutting up these animals, they could learn anything worth knowing, no one would seriously object. Vivisection should be controlled by law.

I believe the time shall come when we shall stop raising failures, when we shall know something of the laws governing human beings. I believe the time will come when we shall not produce deformed persons, natural criminals.

Only those able to raise and educate children should have them. Children should be better born—betted educated.

I look forward to the time when men and women by reason of their knowledge of consequences, of the morality born of intelligence, will refuse to perpetuate disease and pain, will refuse to fill the world with failures.

Nature, so far as we can discern, without passion and without intention, forms, transforms and retransforms forever. She neither weeps nor rejoices. She produces man without purpose and obliterates him without regret. Only through man does Nature take cognizance of the good, the true, and the beautiful. So far as we know man is the highest intelligence. (Ingersoll Memorial Beacon, June 1910 ISH)

Secularism (see also Religion of Humanity)

Secularism is the religion of humanity; it embraces the affairs of this world; it is interested in everything that touches the welfare of a sentient being; it advocates attention to the particular planet on which we happen to live; it means that each individual counts for something; it is a declaration of intellectual independence; it means that the pew is superior to the pulpit, that those who bear the burdens shall have the profits and that they who fill the purse shall hold the strings. It is a protest against ecclesiastical tyranny, against being a serf, subject, or slave of any phantom, or of the priest of any phantom. It is a protest against wasting this life for the sake of one that we know not of. It proposes to let the gods take care of themselves . . . It means living for ourselves and each other; for the present instead of the past, for this world instead of another . . . It is striving to do away with violence and vice, with ignorance, poverty and disease . . . It does not believe in praying and receiving but in earning and deserving . . . It says to the whole world, Work that you may eat, drink and be clothed; work that you may enjoy; work that you may not want; work that you may give and never need.

Separation of Church and State

To Paine, Jefferson and Franklin, we are indebted more than to all others, for a human government, and for a Constitution in which no God is recognized superior to the legally expressed will of the people. They knew that to put God in the Constitution was to put man out. They knew that the recognition of a Deity would be seized upon by fanatics and zealots as a pretext for destroying liberty of thought.

Church and state should be absolutely divorced.

Governors and Presidents should not issue religious proclamations. They should not call upon the people to thank God. It is no part of their official duty. It is outside and beyond the horizon of their authority. There is nothing in the Constitution to justify this religious impertinence.

Only a little while ago, the governor of Minnesota appointed a day of fasting and prayer to see if some power could be induced to kill the grasshoppers or send them in to some other state.

The truth is our government is not founded upon the rights of gods but upon the rights of men. Our Constitution was framed not to declare the deity of Christ, but the sacredness of humanity. Ours is the first government made by the people for the people. It is the only nation in which the gods have had nothing to do.

The God-In-The-Constitution association is weak and fanatical, stupid and absurd. What God are we to have in the Constitution? Whose God? If we should agree tomorrow to put God in the Constitution, the question would then be: Which God? On that question the religious world would fall out. In that direction there is no danger.

Only a few days ago our President by proclamation, thanked God for giving us the victory at Santiago. He did not thank him for sending the yellow fever. To be consistent the President should have thanked him equally for both.

Take from orthodox Christianity the protection of the law, and all church property would be taxed like other property.

The Methodist Church ought not to be sustained by taxation, nor any Catholic, nor any other church. To relieve their property from taxation is to appropriate money, to the extent of the tax, for the support of that church. Whenever a burden is lifted from one piece of property, it is distributed over the rest of the property of the State, and to release one kind of property is to increase the tax on all other kinds ... To exempt the church from taxation is to pay a part of the priest's salary ... In my judgement, every church should be taxed precisely the same as other property ... All institutions for the care of unfortunate people should be secular—should be supported by the state. The money for the purpose should be raised by taxation ...

As long as we have free speech and a free press I think there is no danger of the country being ruled by any church ... I want no man persecuted because of his religion.

We want to do what we can to compel every church to pay taxes on its property as other people pay on theirs ... If you want to build churches, pay taxes. If you want to build a hall or temple in which Freethought and science are to be taught, pay taxes. Let there be no property untaxed. When you fail to tax any species of property, you increase the tax of other people owning the rest. To that extent, you unite church and state . . . We do not wish to employ any chaplains in the navy or in the army, or in the Legislatures or in Congress. It is useless to ask God to help the political party that happens to be in power. We want no President, no Governor "clothed with a little brief authority", to issue a proclamation as though he were an agent of God, authorized to tell all his loving subjects to fast on a certain day, or to enter their churches and pray for the accomplishment of a certain object. It is none of his business.

Jefferson, when President, refused to issue what is known as a "Thanksgiving Proclamation", on the ground that the Federal Government had no right to interfere in religious matters; that the people owed no religious duties to the government; that the government derived its powers, not from priests or gods but from the people, and was responsible alone to the source of its power. The truth is that the framers of our Constitution intended that the government should be secular in the broadest and best sense; and yet there are thousands and thousands of religious people in this country who are greatly scandalized because there is no recognition of God in the Federal Constitution . . . for several years a great many ministers have been endeavoring to have the Constitution amended so as to recognize the existence of God and the divinity of Christ. A man by the name of Pollock was once superintendent of the mint in Philadelphia. He was almost insane about having God in the Constitution. Failing in that, he got the inscription on our money, "In God We Trust". As our silver dollar is now, in fact, worth only eighty-five cents, it is claimed that the inscription means that we trust in God for the other fifteen cents.

The framers of our Constitution wished forever to divorce church and state.

Slavery

I do not believe in a slave-holding God!

Slavery was the bond and pledge of peace, of union, and national greatness. The temple of American liberty was finished—the auction block was the corner stone.

Think of how long we clung to the institution of human slavery, how long lashes upon the naked back were legal tender for the labor performed. Think of it. The pulpit of this country deliberately and willingly, for a hundred years, turned the cross of Christ into a whipping post.

For the purpose of preserving that infinite outrage, words and phrases were warped and stretched, and tortured and thumbscrewed, and racked. Slavery was the one sacred thing, and the Supreme Court was its constitutional guardian.

The entire country was responsible for slavery, and slavery was responsible for rebellion.

In 1833, the USA was the greatest slave-holding power in the civilized world.

The Fugitive Slave Law is the most infamous enactment that ever disgraced a statute book. The man who approves or apologizes for that infamy is a brute.

Before the adoption of the Thirteenth Amendment, the Constitution had always been construed to be the perfect shield of slavery. Freedom was regarded as local prejudice, slavery as the ward of the nation, the jewel of the Constitution.

We must admit that slavery is immoral.

Smoking/Tobacco

Editor's Note: Ingersoll loved cigars. He also rode in the "smoker" when travelling by train which he did very frequently. A chance meeting with a youthful tobacco salesman led to an amusing development. The young man confessed that he was not a very good salesman though he worked hard at his trade. He was married and had children and was worried as to his future in the tobacco business. Very earnestly he asked Ingersoll if he might use his name and picture on a cigar. Ingersoll laughed and allowed that he had no objections if "it's a good cigar." Encouraged, the salesman then asked for an appropriate slogan for the new line of cigars. Without hesitation Ingersoll replied, "How about, 'Let us smoke in this world—not in the next!'" The car rocked with laughter. Several years later the young man was in New York City and looked Ingersoll up. He was a man of modest means now, thanks to the Colonel's endorsement. (Reported by I. Newton Baker in "Robert Green Ingersoll: An Intimate Portrait," C. P. Farell, 1920)

Spiritual/Spirituality (see also Religion of Humanity)

What is it to be spiritual? To recognize the finer harmonies of conduct—to live to the ideal—to separate the incidental, the evanescent, from the perpetual—to be enchanted with the perfect melody of truth—open to the influences of the artistic, the beautiful, the heroic—to shed kindness as the sun sheds light—to recognize the good in others, and to include the world in the idea of self—this is to be spiritual.

There is nothing spiritual in the worship of the unknown and unknowable, in the self-denial of a slave at the command of a master whom he fears. Fastings, prayings, mutilations, kneelings, and mortification are either the results of, or result in, insanity. This is the spirituality of Bedlam, and is of no kindred with the soul that finds its greatest joy in the discharge of obligation perceived.

The spiritual man lives to his ideal. He endeavors to make others happy. He does not despise the passions that have filled the world with art and glory. He loves his wife and children—home and fireside. He cultivates the amenities and refinements of life. He is the friend and the champion of the oppressed. His sympathies are with the poor and suffering. He attacks what he believes to be wrong, though defended by many, and he is willing to stand for the right against the world. He enjoys the beautiful. In the presence of the highest creations of Art his eyes are suffused with tears. When he listens to the great melodies, the divine harmonies, he feels the sorrows and the raptures of death and love. He is intensely human. He carries in his heart the burdens of the world. He searches for the deeper meanings. He appreciates the harmonies of conduct, the melody of a perfect life. He loves his wife and children better than any god. He cares more for the world he lives in than any other. He tries to discharge the duties of this life, to help those that he can reach. He believes in being useful—in making money to feed and clothe and educate the ones he loves—to assist the deserving and to support himself. He is just, generous and sincere. Spirituality is all of this world. It is a child of this earth, born, and cradled here. It comes from no heaven, but it makes a heaven where it is . . . In all relations of life he is faithful and true. He asks for nothing he does not earn. He does not wish to be happy in heaven if he must receive happiness as alms. He does not rely on the goodness of another. He is not anxious to become a winged pauper.

I have not the slightest confidence in "spiritual manifestations" and do not believe that any message has ever been received from the dead.

Straw Man (The)

Some of the preachers who have answered me say that I am fighting a man of straw. I am fighting the supernatural—the dogma of inspiration—the belief in devils—the atonement, salvation by faith—the forgiveness of sins and the savagery of eternal pain. I am fighting the absurd, the monstrous, the cruel. The ministers pretend that they have advanced—that they do not believe the things that I attack. In this they are not honest. Who is the "man of straw"? The man of straw is their master. In every orthodox pulpit stands this man of straw—stands beside the preacher—stands with a club, called a "creed", in his upraised hand. The shadow of this club falls athwart the open Bible—falls upon the preacher's brain, darkens the light of his reason and compels him to betray himself.

Suicide as Euthanasia

There are circumstances in which suicide is natural, sensible, and right. When a man is of no use to himself, when he can be of no use to others, when his life is filled with agony, when the future has no promise of relief, then I think he has the right to cast the burden of life away and seek the repose of death.

There is no relationship between the suicides and killing idiots. Suicide may, under certain conditions, be right and killing idiots may be wrong; killing idiots may be right and suicide may be wrong. When we look about us, when we read interviews with preachers about Jonah, we know that all of the idiots have not been killed.

When some suffering wretch, wild with pain, crazed with regret, frenzied with fear, with desperate hand unties the knot of life, let us have pity. Let us be generous.

Every man of sense knows that a person being devoured by cancer has the right to take morphine, and pass from agony to dreamless sleep. So too, there are circumstances under which a man has the right to end his pain of mind.

Is suicide justifiable? Certainly. When a man is useless to himself and to others he has the right to determine what he will do about living . . . I don't take into consideration any supernatural nonsense. If God wants a man to stay here he ought to make it more comfortable for him.

Sunday Closing Laws

I hope to live until all these foolish laws are repealed and until we are in the highest and noblest sense a free people. And by free I mean each having the right to do anything that does not interfere with the rights or with the happiness of another. I want to see the time when we live for this world and when all shall endeavor to increase, by education, by reason, and by persuasion, the sum of human happiness . . . Nothing can be more absurd than the idea that any particular space of time is sacred. Everything in nature goes on the same on Sunday as on other days, and if beyond nature there is a God, then God works on Sunday as he does on all other days. There is no rest in nature. The old idea that God made the world and then rested is idiotic.

I think all days, all times and all seasons are alike sacred. I think the best day in a man's life is the day that he is truly happiest. Every day in which good is done to humanity is a holy day . . . A space of time cannot be sacred, any more than a vacuum can be sacred, and it is rendered sacred by deeds done in it, and not in and of itself. If we should finally invent some means of travelling by which we could go a thousand miles a day, a man could escape Sunday all his life by travelling West. He could start Monday, and stay Monday all the time. Or, if he should some time get near the North Pole, he could walk faster than the earth turns and thus beat Sunday all the while.

I think that all days are substantially alike in the long run. It is no worse to drink on Sunday than on Monday. The idea that one day in the week is holy is wholly idiotic. Besides, these closing laws do no good . . . Ever since I can remember people have been trying to make other people temperate by intemperate laws.

Of course, the idea that one day is better than another is infinitely absurd—that a space of time can be "holy", or that man is under any more obligation one day than another, to do good, to love mercy, and to increase the happiness of his fellow man. All things that man ought to do on any day of the week, certainly can be done on Sunday, without sin. The whole matter may be summed up thus: It is never right to do wrong, and it is never wrong to do right. (Letters, p. 334)

Supernatural

As to the existence of the supernatural, one man knows precisely as much, and exactly as little as another. Upon this question, chimpanzees and cardinals, apes and popes are upon exact equality.

Whatever idea there is must have been a natural product. As a consequence of this, there can be no supernatural idea in the human brain . . . there is no supernatural idea in the human brain . . . Man gets all food for thought through the medium of the senses. . . . All food for thought, then, is natural.

My belief is that the supernatural has had its day. The church must either change or abdicate. That is to say, it must keep step with the progress of the world or be trampled under foot. The church as a power has ceased to exist.

Being satisfied that the supernatural does not exist, man should turn his entire attention to the affairs of this world, to the facts of nature. And first of all, he should avoid waste—waste of energy, waste of wealth. Every good man, every good woman, should try to do away with war, to stop the appeal to savage force.

Toleration

For one man to say to another, "I tolerate you" is an assumption of superiority, and it is not a disclaimer but a waiver of the right to persecute. (ISH Col.)

Unitarians, Universalists

Do not forget to say that I mean orthodox churches, orthodox clergy, because I have great respect for Unitarians and Universalists.

The Unitarian church has done more than any other church—and may be more than all other churches—to substitute character for creed . . . I want to thank the Unitarian Church for what it has done. I want to thank the Universalist Church too. They at least believe in a God who is a gentleman . . . they believe, at least, in a heavenly father who will leave the latch string out until the last child gets home.

Editor's Note: The proceeds from Ingersoll's second public lecture went to refurnishing the interior of the Universalist Church of Peoria, Illinois. (Chicago Tribune, 7-22-99)

U.S. Postal Service

We do not carry the mail in a State because it pays. We carry it because there are people there; because there are American citizens there; not because it pays. The post office is not a miser; it is a national benefactor. There are only seventeen states in this Union where the income of the Post Office Department is equal to the outlay . . . There are twenty-one states in which the mail is carried at a loss.

In 1851 the postage was reduced to three cents when it was prepaid, and the law provided that the diminution of income should not discontinue any route, neither should it affect the establishment of new routes, and for the first time in the history of our Government the idea of productiveness was abandoned. It was not a question of whether we would make money or not; the question was, did the people deserve a mail and was it in the interest of the Government to carry that mail? I am a believer in the diffusion of intelligence. I believe in frequent mails.

When One Line Was Enough!

Age discards the superfluous, the immaterial straw and chaff, and hoards the golden grain.

Everything of beauty tends to the elevation of man.

The brain wants light; the heart wants love.

One biscuit, with plenty of butter, is worth all the tracts ever distributed.

Calvinism was the child of indigestion.

Nothing discloses character like the use of power.

I stand by the dogma of demonstration.

I believe in no charity that is founded on robbery.

I have no great confidence in organized charities.

Desires betray the judgement and cunningly mislead the will.

The falling leaf that tells of autumn's death is, in a subtler sense, a prophesy of spring.

Fear paints pictures of ghosts and hangs them in the gallery of ignorance.

The road is short to anything we fear.

I think it much better to feed the hungry than to starve yourself.

I am not so much for the freedom of religion as I am for the religion of freedom.

Free thought will give us truth.

Genius has the climate of perpetual growth.

The grave is not a throne; the corpse is not a king.

It is hard to live a great while without growing old, and it is hardly worthwhile to die just to keep young.

Great men, after all, are the instrumentalities of their time.

Good character is not the work of a day; it is the work of a life.

Happiness dwells in the valleys with the shadows.

Heresy extends the hospitality of the brain to a new thought.

Heresy is a cradle; orthodoxy a coffin.

Hope is the only bee that makes honey without flowers.

The human race cannot afford to exchange its liberty for any possible comfort.

They who demand hypocrisy must be satisfied with mediocrity.

Ignorance is the only shield to protect you from the wrath of God.

A known infidel cannot get very rich, for the reason that the Christians are so forgiving and loving that they boycott him.

Infidels in all ages have battled for the rights of man, and have at all times been the fearless advocates of liberty and justice.

Intellectual freedom is only the right to be honest.

Every man who expresses an honest thought is a soldier in the army of intellectual liberty.

In the intellectual sea there is room for every sail.

Kindness is always evidence of greatness.

Laughter lengthens life.

The law's delay is more often the lawyer's delay and should not be tolerated.

Liberty is the birthright of all.

A library is an arsenal.

A life should not be written until it has been lived.

The living have the right to control this world.

Malice is the property of small souls.

You cannot make a prison out of a presumption any more than you can make a gibbet out of suspicion.

After all, man and woman are the highest possible titles.

Now and then there arises a man who on peril's edge draws from the scabbard of despair the sword of victory.

Man naturally rushes from one extreme to another.

Memory is the miser of the mind; forgetfulness the spendthrift.

Morality is the harmony between act and circumstances; it is the melody of conduct.

I will pay a premium of one thousand dollars a word for each and every word I ever said or wrote in favor of sending obscene publications through the mails.

Old age should enjoy the luxury of giving.

People should marry because it increases the happiness of each and all.

I do not think the Republican Party should again nominate Rutherford B. Hayes; I do not think he could win if nobody ran against him.

Religion is a kind of disease.

How can we get along without the revelation that no one understands?

He has placed himself beyond the reach of ridicule.

Salvation for credulity means damnation for investigation.

Shakespeare is my Bible and Burns my hymnbook!

The distance from Shakespeare must be measured not by hundreds, but by millions of years.

Sleep is the best medicine in the world.

A smile is the dawn of a doubt.

If thirteen is a dangerous number, twenty-six ought to be twice as dangerous, and fifty-two, four times as terrible.

All the fields of space are sown thick with constellations.

Spain has always been exceedingly religious and extremely cruel.

The sun shines as gladly on the coffin as on the cradle.

Superstition is, always has been, and forever will be, the foe of progress, the enemy of education and the assassin of freedom.

In every man's pathway hiss and writhe the serpents of suspicion.

Suspicion is the soil in which prejudice grows.

Truth is made no worse by the one who tells it, and a lie gets no real benefit from the reputation of its author.

The man who finds a truth lights a torch.

Vice either lives before Love is born, or after Love is dead.

Wine is a fireside and whiskey a conflagration.

Words are the garments of thoughts, the robes of ideas.

Good, honest, faithful work is worship.

Youth has a wish—old age a dread.

It is hard to overstate the debt that we owe to men and women of genius.

"Col., if you had been in charge of creation, what would you have done differently?" Well, first of all, I would have made good health "catching" instead of disease.

Nothing, as a raw material, is a decided failure!

Woman/Women

In the olden times when religions were manufactured—when priestcraft and lunacy governed the world—the women were not consulted. They were regarded and treated as serfs and menials—looked upon as a species of property to be bought and sold like other domestic animals.

Women have been treated like poisonous beasts.

Women have through many generations, acquired the habit of submission, of acquiescence. They have practiced what may be called the slave virtues—obedience, humility—so that some time will be required for them to become accustomed to the new order of things, to the exercise of greater freedom. So, I say, equal rights, equal education, equal advantages.

In every field where woman has become a competitor of man she has either become or given evidence that she is to become, his equal. My own opinion is that woman is naturally the equal of man and that in time, that is to say, when she has had the opportunity and the training, she will produce in the world of art as great pictures, as great statues, and in the world of literature as great books, dramas, and poetry as man has produced or will produce.

I think the influence of women is always good, in politics, as in everything else. I think it is the duty of every woman to ascertain what she can in regard to her country, including its history, its laws and customs. Woman above all others is a teacher. She, above all, determines the character of children, that is to say of men and women. There is not the slightest danger of women becoming too intellectual or knowing too much. Neither is there any danger of men knowing too much. At least, I know of no men who are in immediate peril from that source. I am a firm believer in the equal rights of human beings, and no matter what I think as to what woman should or should not do, she has the same right to decide for herself that I have to decide for myself. If women wish to vote, if they wish to take part in political matters, if they wish to run for office, I shall do nothing to interfere with their rights. I most cheerfully admit that my political rights are only equal to theirs.

Think of making your wife a beggar! Think of her having to ask you every day for a dollar, or for two dollars, or fifty cents! "What did you do with that dollar I gave you last week?" Think of having a wife that is afraid of you! What kind of children do you expect to have with a beggar and a coward for their mother?

Editor's Note: In this regard the reader should know that Ingersoll himself simply put money in a cashbox in his house and every member of the family helped herself.

In my judgement, the woman is the equal of the man. She has all the rights I have and one more, and that is the right to be protected. If there is any man I detest, it is the man who thinks he is the head of a family—the man who thinks he is "boss".

Women are not willing to suffer here, with the hope of being happy beyond the clouds. They want their happiness now. They are beginning to think for themselves.

I regard the rights of men and women equal. In Love's fair realm, husband and wife are king and queen, sceptered and crowned alike, and seated on the selfsame throne.

The gentlemen of today show more affection for their dogs than most of the kings of England exhibited toward their wives.

Look at the women in this town sewing for a living, making cloaks for less than forty-five cents that sell for forty-five dollars! Right here (New York City) amid all the palaces, amid the thousands and millions of property—here! Is that all civilization can do? Must a woman support herself, or her child, or her children, by that kind of labor, and with such pay?

Most women are driven at last to the sewing needle, and this does not allow them to live. It simply keeps them from dying. No girl is safe in the streets of any city after the sun has gone down. After all, the sun is the only god that has ever protected woman. In the darkness she has been the prey of the wild beast in man.

I am willing that every woman in the nation who desires the privilege and honor shall vote. If any woman wants to vote, I am too much of a gentleman to say she shall not. She gets her right, if she has it, from precisely the same source that I get mine. There are many questions upon which I deem it desirable that women should vote, especially upon the question of peace and war.

I think the women who have been engaged in the struggle for equal rights have done good for women in the direction of obtaining equal wages for equal work. There has also been a tendency among women in our country to become independent—a desire to make their own living—to win their own bread.

The men who declare that woman is the intellectual inferior of man, do not and cannot, by offering themselves in evidence, substantiate their declaration.

Husbands as a rule, do not know a great deal, and it will not do for every wife to depend on the ignorance of her worst half. The women of today are the great readers, and no book is a great success unless it pleases the women.

No woman should be forced to live with a man whom she

abhors. There never will be a free generation of great men until there has been a generation of free women—of free mothers.

Nothing gives me more pleasure, nothing gives greater promise for the future than the fact that woman is achieving intellectual and physical liberty. It is refreshing to know that here, in our country, there are thousands of women who think and express their own thoughts—who are thoroughly free and thoroughly conscientious. Woman is not the intellectual inferior of man.

The crosses of this world are mostly borne by wives, by mothers and by daughters. Their brows are pierced by thorns. They shed the bitterest tears. They live and suffer and die for others. It is almost enough to make one insane to think of what woman, in the years of savagery and civilization has suffered. Think of the anxiety and agony of motherhood. Maternity is the most pathetic fact in the universe. Think how helpless girls are. Think of the thorns in the paths they walk—of the trials, the temptations, the want, the misfortune, the dangers and anxieties that fill their days and nights. Every true man will sympathize with woman, and will do all in his power to lighten her burdens and increase the sunshine in her life.

Editor's Note: One time while in Chicago for a lecture tour, Ingersoll was staying at the Palmer House. As always, he was the favorite copy of newspapermen. He never tired of giving interviews, enjoying himself immensely. A bellboy came to his room and presented him with a card which indicated that a young woman on her first assignment wanted to interview the Colonel and Mrs. Ingersoll. He invited her up. No matter how gracious her reception, the cub reporter was very nervous. Ingersoll put her at her ease. He declared, "I'm glad they sent a woman. I'm tired of men reporters. Just fire ahead with your questions and we'll fix up an interview that will make the men ashamed of themselves." The reporter, relieved, wrote her interview and was rewarded with two free tickets to the evening lecture and an invitation from Mrs. Ingersoll to drop in again.

Science must make woman the owner, the mistress of herself. Science, the only possible saviour of mankind, must put it in the power of woman to decide for herself whether she will or will not become a mother. This is the solution of the whole question. This frees woman. The babes that are born will be welcome. They will be clasped with glad hands to happy breasts. They will fill homes with light and joy.

Editor's Note: In his speeches, Ingersoll invariably employed the word *man* as an all-inclusive designation for the human species. In the desire for economy of words, to avoid awkwardness, plus the long-established custom in regard to usage, Ingersoll used the word *man* as a synonym for humanity, not male. The reader will discover that if Ingersoll had any prejudice at all, it was that he regarded women in general the superior to men in general.

As long as woman regards the Bible as the charter of her rights, she will be the slave of man. The Bible was not written by a woman. Within its lids there is nothing but humiliation and shame. She is regarded as the property of man.

Man having been the physical superior of woman always accounts for the fact that most of the high gods have been males. Had woman been the physical superior, the powers supposed to be the rulers of Nature would have been women. Instead of being represented in the apparel of man, they would be luxuriated in trains, low-necked dresses, laces and black hair.

If we wish to find what the Bible thinks of woman, all that is necessary to do is read it. We will find everywhere she is spoken of simply as property—as belonging absolutely to the man. We will find that whenever a man got tired of his wife, all he had to do was give her a writing of divorcement, and that then the mother of his children became a houseless and homeless wanderer. We will find that men were allowed to have as many wives as they could get, either by courtship, purchase, or conquest.

Nearly every religion has accounted for all the devilment of this world by the crime of a woman. What a gallant thing that is. And if it be true, I had rather live with the woman I love in a world full of trouble, than to live in heaven with nobody but men.

Ingersoll.   Courtesy Illinois State Historical Library.

Courtesy Illinois State Historical Library.

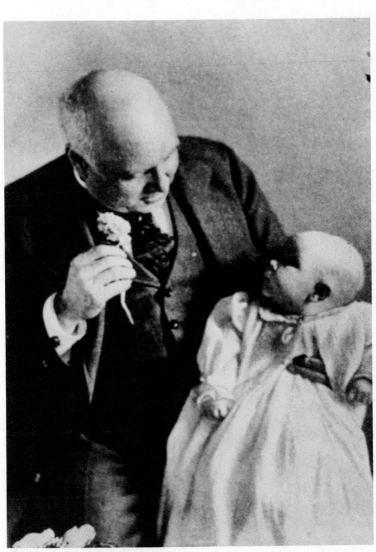

Ingersoll and Granddaughter.
Courtesy Illinois State Historical Library.

Ingersoll and Granddaughter Eva and Grandson Robert.
Courtesy Illinois State Historical Library.

The author at the Ingersoll statue, Glen Oaks Park, Peoria, Illinois.

The Beckwith Memorial Theater Building
Dowagiac, Michigan 1893-1966

Chicago Exposition Building Looking south on Michigan Ave., 1880s.
Courtesy Chicago Historical Society. Credit photographer: J. W. Taylor

Ingersoll's grave at Arlington National Cemetery.

CHAPTER TWO

SPEECHES OF
ROBERT INGERSOLL

A Tribute To Ebon C. Ingersoll*

Washington, D.C., May 31, 1879

DEAR FRIENDS: I am going to do that which the dead oft promised he would do for me.

The loved and loving brother, husband, father, friend, died where manhood's morning almost touches noon, and while the shadows still were falling toward the west.

He had not passed on life's highway the stone that marks the highest point; but being weary for a moment, he lay down by the wayside, and using his burden for a pillow, fell into that dreamless sleep that kisses down his eyelids still. While yet in love with life and raptured with the world, he passed to silence and pathetic dust.

Yet, after all, it may be best, just in the happiest, sunniest hour of all the voyage, while eager winds are kissing every sail, to dash against the unseen rock, and in an instant hear the billows roar above a sunken ship. For whether in mid-sea or 'mong the breakers of the farther shore, a wreck at last must mark the end of each and all. And every life, no matter if its every hour is rich with love and every moment jeweled with a joy, will, at its close, become a tragedy as sad and deep and dark as can be

---

*Ebon Clark Ingersoll was a beloved brother of Robert.

woven of the warp and woof of mystery and death.

This brave and tender man in every storm of life was oak and rock; but in the sunshine he was vine and flower. He was the friend of all heroic souls. He climbed the heights, and left all superstitions far below, while on his forehead fell the golden dawning of the grander day.

He loved the beautiful, and was with color, form and music touched to tears. He sided with the weak, the poor, and wronged, and lovingly gave alms. With loyal heart and with purest hands he faithfully discharged all public trusts.

He was a worshiper of liberty, a friend of the oppressed. A thousand times I have heard him quote these words: "For Justice all place a temple, and all season, summer." He believed that happiness is the only good, reason the only torch, justice the only worship, humanity the only religion, and love the only priest. He added to the sum of human joy; and were every one to whom he did some loving service to bring a blossom to his grave, he would sleep tonight beneath a wilderness of flowers.

Life is a narrow vale between the cold and barren peaks of two eternities. We strive in vain to look beyond the heights. We cry aloud, and the only answer is the echo of our wailing cry. From the voiceless lips of the unreplying dead there comes no word; but in the night of death hope sees a star and listening love can hear the rustle of a wing.

He who sleeps here, when dying, mistaking the approach of death for the return of health, whispered with his latest breath, "I am better now."** Let us believe, in spite of doubts and dogmas, of fears and tears, that these dear words are true of all the countless dead.

The record of a generous life runs like a vine around the memory of our dead, and every sweet unselfish act is now a perfumed flower.

And now, to you, who have been chosen, from among the many men he loved, to do the last sad office for the dead, we give his sacred dust.

Speech cannot contain our love. There was, there is, no gentler, stronger, manlier man.

**These were also R.G.I.'s last words.

At a Child's Grave*

Washington, D.C., January 8, 1882

MY FRIENDS: I know how vain it is to gild a grief with words, and yet I wish to take from every grave its fear. Here in this world, where life and death are equal kings, all should be brave enough to meet what all the dead have met. The future has been filled with fear, stained and polluted by the heartless past. From the wondrous tree of life the buds and blossoms fall with ripened fruit, and in the common bed of earth, patriarchs and babes sleep side by side.

Why should we fear that which will come to all that is? We cannot tell, we do not know, which is the greater blessing—life or death. We cannot say that death is not a good. We do not know whether the grave is the end of this life, or the door of another, or whether the night here is not somewhere else a dawn. Neither can we tell which is the more fortunate—the child dying in its mother's arms, before its lips have learned to form a word, or he who journeys all the length of life's uneven road, painfully taking the last slow steps with staff and crutch.

Every cradle asks us "Whence?" and every coffin "Whither?" The poor barbarian, weeping above his dead, can answer these questions just as well as the robed priest of the most authentic creed. The tearful ignorance of the one, is as consoling as the learned and unmeaning words of the other. No man, standing where the horizon of a life has touched a grave, has any right to prophesy a future filled with pain and tears.

It may be that death gives all there is of worth to life. If those we press and strain within our arms could never die, perhaps that love would wither from the earth. It may be that com-

---

*The "child" was the daughter of a policeman who prevailed upon Ingersoll to give the eulogy. As usual, Ingersoll responded with great eloquence and compassion.

mon fate treads from out the paths between our hearts the weeds of selfishness and hate. And I had rather live and love where death is king, than have eternal life where love is not. Another life is nought, unless we know and love again the ones who love us here.

They who stand with breaking hearts around this little grave, need have no fear. The larger and the nobler faith in all that is, and is to be, tells us that death, even at its worst, is only perfect rest. We know that through the common wants of life—the needs and duties of each hour—their grief will lessen day by day, until at last this grave will be to them a place of rest and peace—almost of joy. There is for them this consolation: The dead do not suffer. If they live again, their lives will surely be as good as ours. We have no fear. We are all children of the same mother, and the same fate awaits us all. We, too, have our religion, and it is this: Help for the living—Hope for the dead.

A Tribute to Henry Ward Beecher*

New York, June 26, 1887

He passed from harsh and cruel creeds to that serene philosophy that has no place for pride or hate, that threatens no revenge, that looks on sin as stumblings of the blind and pities those who fall, knowing that in the souls of all there is a sacred yearning for the light. He ceased to think of man as something thrust upon the world—an exile from some other sphere. He felt at last that men are part of Nature's self—kindred of all life—the gradual growth of countless years; that all the sacred books were helps until outgrown, and all religions rough and devious paths that man has worn with weary feet in sad and painful search for truth and peace. To him these paths were wrong, and yet all gave the promise of success. He knew that all the streams, no matter how they wander, turn and curve amid the hills or rocks, or linger in the lakes and pools, must some time reach the sea. These views enlarged his soul and made him patient with the world, and while the wintry snows of age were falling on his head, Spring, with all her wealth of bloom, was in his heart.

The memory of this ample man is now a part of Nature's wealth. He battled for the rights of men. His heart was with the slave. He stood against the selfish greed of millions banded to protect the pirate's trade. His voice was for the right when freedom's friends were few. He taught the church to think and doubt. He did not fear to stand alone. His brain took counsel of his heart. To every foe he offered reconciliation's hand. He

---

*Ingersoll and Beecher were more than acquaintances. Each had boundless admiration for the other. When Beecher died, Ingersoll delivered a long eulogy from which the concluding paragraphs are presented here.

loved this land of ours, and added to its glory through the world. He was the greatest orator that stood within the pulpit's narrow curve. He loved the liberty of speech. There was no trace of bigot in his blood. He was a brave and generous man.

With reverent hands, I place this tribute on his tomb.

A Tribute to Walt Whitman*

Camden, N.J., March 30, 1892

MY FRIENDS: Again we, in the mystery of Life, are brought face to face with the mystery of Death. A great man, a great American, the most eminent citizen of this Republic, lies dead before us, and we have met to pay a tribute to his greatness and his worth.

I know he needs no words of mine. His fame is secure. He laid the foundation of it deep in the human heart and brain. He was, above all I have known, the poet of humanity, of sympathy. He was so great that he rose above the greatest that he met without arrogance, and so great that he stooped to the lowest without conscious condescension. He never claimed to be lower or greater than any of the sons of men.

He came into our generation a free, untrammeled spirit, with sympathy for all. His arm was beneath the form of the sick. He sympathized with the imprisoned and despised, and even on the brow of crime he was great enough to place the kiss of human sympathy.

One of the greatest lines in our literature is his, and the line is great enough to do honor to the greatest genius that has ever lived. He said, speaking of an outcast: "Not til the sun excludes you do I exclude you."

His charity was as wide as the sky, and wherever there was human suffering, human misfortune, the sympathy of Whitman bent above it as the firmament bends above the earth.

He was built on a broad and splendid plan—ample, without appearing to have limitations—passing easily for a brother of mountains and seas and constellations; caring nothing for the little maps and charts with which timid pilots hug the shore, but giving himself freely with recklessness of genius to winds and

---

*Years later, and in direct reference to this eulogy, Carl Sandburg declared, "Ingersoll on Whitman is a precious thing, a treasure."

waves and tides; caring for nothing as long as the stars were above him. He walked among men, among writers, among verbal varnishers and veneerers, among literary milliners and tailors, with the unconscious majesty of an antique god.

He was the poet of that divine democracy which gives equal rights to all the sons and daughters of men. He uttered the great American voice; uttered a song worthy of the great Republic. No man ever said more for the rights of humanity, more in favor of real democracy, of real justice. He neither scorned nor cringed, was neither tyrant nor slave. He asked only to stand the equal of his fellows beneath the great flag of nature, the blue and stars.

He was the poet of Life. It was a joy simply to breathe. He loved the clouds; he enjoyed the breath of morning, the twilight, the wind, the winding streams. He loved to look at the sea when the waves burst into the whitecaps of joy. He loved the fields, the hills; he was acquainted with the trees, with birds, with all the beautiful objects of the earth. He not only saw these objects, but understood their meaning, and he used them that he might exhibit his heart to his fellowmen.

He was the poet of Love. He was not ashamed of that divine passion that has built every home in the world; that divine passion that has painted every picture and given us every real work of art; that divine passion that has made the world worth living in and has given some value to human life.

He was the poet of the natural, and taught men not to be ashamed of that which is natural. He was not only the poet of democracy, not only the poet of the great Republic, but he was the poet of the human race. He was not confined to the limits of this country, but his sympathy went out over the seas to all the nations of the earth.

He stretched out his hand and felt himself the equal of all kings and of all princes, and the brother of all men, no matter how high, no matter how low.

He has uttered more supreme words than any writer of our century, possibly of almost any other. He was, above all things, a man, and above genius, above all the snow-capped peaks of intelligence, above all art, rises the true man. Greater than all is the true man, and he walked among his fellowmen as such.

He was the poet of Death. He accepted all life and all death, and he justified all. He had the courage to meet all, and was great enough and splendid enough to harmonize all and to accept all there is of life as a divine melody.

You know better than I what his life has been, but let me say one thing. Knowing, as he did, what others can know and what they cannot, he accepted and absorbed all theories, all creeds, all religions, and believed in none. His philosophy was a sky that embraced all clouds and accounted for all clouds. He had a philosophy and a religion of his own, broader, as he believed—and as I believe—than others. He accepted all, he understood all, and he was above all.

He was absolutely true to himself. He had frankness and courage, and he was as candid as light. He was willing that all the sons of men should be absolutely acquainted with his heart and brain. He had nothing to conceal. Frank, candid, pure, serene, noble, and yet for years he was maligned and slandered, simply because he had the candor of nature. He will be understood yet, and that for which he was condemned—his frankness, his candor—will add to the glory and the greatness of his fame.

He wrote a liturgy for mankind; he wrote a great and splendid psalm of life, and he gave to us the gospel of humanity—the greatest gospel that can be preached.

He was not afraid to live, not afraid to die. For many years he and death were near neighbors. He was always willing and ready to meet and greet this king called death, and for many months he sat in the deepening twilight waiting for the night, waiting for the light.

He never lost his hope. When the mists filled the valleys, he looked upon the mountain tops, and when the mountains in darkness disappeared, he fixed his gaze upon the stars.

In his brain were the blessed memories of the day, and in his heart were mingled the dawn and dusk of life.

He was not afraid; he was cheerful every moment. The laughing nymphs of day did not desert him. They remained that they might clasp the hands and greet with smiles the veiled and silent sisters of the night. And when they did come, Walt Whitman stretched his hand to them. On one side were the nymphs of the day, and on the other the silent sisters of the night, and so, hand in hand, between smiles and tears, he reached his journey's end.

From the frontier of life, from the western wave-kissed shore, he sent us messages of content and hope, and these messages seem now like strains of music blown by the "Mystic-Trumpeter" from Death's pale realm.

Today we give back to Mother Nature, to her clasp and kiss, one of the bravest sweetest souls that ever lived in human clay.

Charitable as the air and generous as Nature, he was negligent of all except to do and say what he believed he should do and should say.

And I today thank him, not only for you but for myself, for all the brave words he has uttered. I thank him for all the great and splendid words he has said in favor of liberty, in favor of man and woman, in favor of motherhood, in favor of fathers, in favor of children, and I thank him for the brave words that he has said of death.

He has lived, he has died, and death is less terrible than it was before. Thousands and millions will walk down into the "dark valley of the shadow" holding Walt Whitman by the hand. Long after we are dead the brave words he has spoken will sound like trumpets to the dying.

And so I lay this little wreath upon this great man's tomb. I loved him living, and I love him still.

A Tribute to Philo D. Beckwith*

Dowagiac, Mich., January 25, 1893

LADIES AND GENTLEMEN: Nothing is nobler than to plant the flower of gratitude on the grave of a generous man—of one who labored for the good of all—whose hands were open and whose heart was full.

Praise for the noble dead is an inspiration for the noble living.

Loving words sow seeds of love in every gentle heart. Ap-

---

*Some time ago in Dowagiac, Mich., died Philo D. Beckwith, a man of broad views and great business capacity . . . .

This little but bustling village will become artistically famous through P. D. Beckwith who practically originated it.

He made a great fortune here, but he lost no kindness of heart with the acquisition of money. During the latter part of his life he expressed a desire to erect in this town a theatre that would insure to his fellow-townsmen the very best of attractions, irrespective of the very small offering that the place would naturally make to the greater stars and companies. Money-making did not enter into Mr. Beckwith's plan. He was willing to pay the deficit that it involved.

He died before he could put his purpose into execution. But his heirs have carried out his wishes to the letter; and Dowagiac now boasts one of the handsomest theatres of its size in the world, while the endowment for its support will insure its use as its noble projector planned. The building is a plain structure exteriorly, of red pressed brick and brown stone trimmings. A noble exterior feature, however, is a frieze of portraits in terra-cotta bas-reliefs of eminent writers, philosophers, artists and actors.

The collection favors those of broad religious views. Mr. Beckwith was a great admirer of Thomas Paine, Voltaire and Robert G. Ingersoll—who recently delivered an address upon Shakespeare at the formal dedication of this theatre—and in this frieze are Shakespeare, Ingersoll, Voltaire, Thomas Paine, . . . and others.
—New York Dramatic Mirror, February 1893.

preciation is the soil and climate of good and generous deeds.

We are met tonight not to pay, but to acknowledge a debt of gratitude to one who lived and labored here—who was the friend of all and who for many years was the providence of the poor. To one who left to those who knew him best the memory of countless loving deeds—the richest legacy that man can leave to man.

We are here to dedicate this monument to the stainless memory of Philo D. Beckwith—one of the kings of men.

This monument—this perfect theatre—this beautiful house of cheerfulness and joy—this home and child of all the arts—this temple where the architect, the sculptor and painter united to build and decorate a stage whereon the drama with a thousand tongues will tell the frailties and the virtues of the human race, and music with her thrilling voice will touch the source of happy tears.

This is a fitting monument to the man whose memory we honor—to one, who broadening with the years, outgrew the cruel creeds, the heartless dogmas of his time—to one who passed from superstition to science—from religion to reason—from theology to humanity—from slavery to freedom—from the shadow of fear to the blessed light of love and courage. To one who believed in intellectual hospitality—in the perfect freedom of the soul, and hated tyranny, in every form, with all his heart.

To one whose head and hands were in partnership constituting the firm of Intelligence and Industry, and whose heart divided the profits with his fellowmen. To one who fought the battle of life alone, without the aid of place or wealth, and yet grew nobler and gentler with success.

To one who tried to make a heaven here and who believed in the blessed gospel of cheerfulness and love—of happiness and hope.

And it is fitting, too, that this monument should be adorned with the sublime faces, wrought in stone, of the immortal dead—of those who battled for the rights of man—who broke the fetters of the slave—of those who filled the minds of men with poetry, art, and light—of Voltaire, who abolished torture in France and who did more for liberty than any other of the sons of men—of Thomas Paine, whose pen did as much as any sword to make the New World free—of Victor Hugo, who wept for those who weep—of Emerson, a worshiper of the Ideal, who filled the mind with suggestions of the perfect—of Goethe, the poet-philosopher—of Whitman, the ample, wide as the sky—author of the tenderest, the most pathetic, the sublimest poem that this continent has produced—of Shakespeare, the King of all—of Beethoven, the divine,—of Chopin and Verdi and of Wagner, grandest of them all, whose music satisfies the heart and brain and fills imagination's sky—of George Eliot, who wove within her brain the purple robe her genius wears—of George Sand, subtle and sincere, passionate and free—and with these—faces of those who, on the stage, have made the mimic world as real as life and death.

Beneath the loftiest monuments may be found ambition's worthless dust, while those who lived the loftiest lives are sleeping now in unknown graves.

It may be that the bravest of the brave who ever fell upon the field of ruthless war, was left without a grave to mingle slowly with the land he saved.

But here and now the man and monument agree, and blend like sounds that meet and melt in melody—a monument for the dead—a blessing for the living—a memory of tears—a prophecy of joy.

Fortunate the people where this good man lived, for they are all his heirs—and fortunate for me that I have had the privilege of laying this little laurel leaf upon his unstained brow.

And now, speaking for those he loved—for those who represent the honored dead—I dedicate this home of mirth and song—of poetry and art—to the memory of Philo D. Beckwith—a true philosopher—a real philanthropist.

Editor's Note: The reader should be reminded that following this tribute, given without notes or pause, was a three-hour lecture on Shakespeare, again without notes or pause. It is reported that not one in attendance left prior to the conclusion of the lecture!

At the Tomb of Napoleon

Editor's Note: When Ingersoll went to Europe he visited the usual "shrines" and had comments for one and all. Perhaps the most famous and lasting commentary he gave was in response to a reporter's question, "What do you think of Napoleon's tomb?" His reply was later incorporated into one of Ingersoll's favorite lectures, "The Liberty of Man, Woman and Child."

A little while ago, I stood by the grave of the old Napoleon—a magnificent tomb of gilt and gold, fit almost for a dead deity—and gazed upon the sarcophagus of rare and nameless marble, where rest at last the ashes of that restless man. I leaned over the balustrade and thought about the career of the greatest soldier of the modern world.

I saw him walking upon the banks of the Seine, contemplating suicide. I saw him at Toulon—I saw him putting down the mob in the streets of Paris—I saw him at the head of the army of Italy—I saw him crossing the bridge of Lodi with the tri-color in his hand—I saw him conquer the Alps and mingle the eagles of France with the eagles of the crags. I saw him at Marengo—at Ulm and Austerlitz. I saw him in Russia, where the infantry of the snow and the cavalry of the wild blast scattered his legions like winter's withered leaves. I saw him at Leipsic in defeat and disaster—driven by a million bayonets back upon Paris—clutched like a wild beast—banished to Elba. I saw him escape and retake an empire by the force of his genius. I saw him upon the frightful field of Waterloo, where Chance and Fate combined to wreck the fortunes of their former king. And I saw him at St. Helena, with his hands crossed behind him, gazing out upon the sad and solemn sea.

I thought of the orphans and widows he had made—of the tears that had been shed for his glory, and of the only woman who ever loved him, pushed from his heart by the cold hand of ambition. And I said I would rather have been a French peasant and worn wooden shoes. I would rather have lived in a hut with a vine growing over the door, and the grapes growing purple in the kisses of the autumn sun. I would rather have been that poor peasant with my loving wife by my side, knitting as the day died out of the sky—with my children upon my knees and their arms about me—I would rather have been that man and gone down to the tongueless silence of the dreamless dust, than to have been that imperial impersonation of force and murder, known as "Napoleon the Great."

APPENDIX I
THE FINEST
THEATER IN AMERICA

It was said to be, "the finest theater in America." It was built in 1892 at the then astounding cost of one hundred thousand dollars! Today, to build an exact duplicate of the Beckwith Memorial Theater Building would require an expenditure of approximately one and a half million dollars. In its heyday, the great and near-great graced its handsome, spacious stage. Among the notables who appeared at Beckwith were: Jenny Lind, John Drew, T. S. Hart, Madame Rhea, Otis Skinner, May Robsen, Lewis & Stone, Fisk O'Hara, Robert Mantell, Walker Whitside, and Ethel Barrymore. This is but a "sampling" of the giants of theater who welcomed the opportunity to "play" the Beckwith Theater. Unusual as the Beckwith was for the quality of its construction, its location made it all the more remarkable. Enter Dowagiac, Michigan. In 1892 its population was approximately seven thousand. Its population today: approximately seven thousand.

Why, in the 1890s, would anyone in full control of his faculties lavish a hundred thousand dollar extravagance on little Dowagiac of southwestern Michigan? How did it come to pass that Dowagiac could actually boast of "the finest theater of its size in the United States"? While poring through *The Complete Works of Robert Green Ingersoll* (Farrell & Co., 1900, in twelve volumes), I came upon a tribute delivered by Ingersoll to the beloved memory of one Philo D. Beckwith. That date was January 25, 1893; the place, Dowagiac's brand new Beckwith Memorial Theater. As Dowagiac is but an hour's drive from my home, I drove there: the adventure had begun. That first trip was but an introduction. Over the next two months, I would be in Dowagiac at least weekly.

My interest in the Beckwith Theater had begun in volume 12 of Ingersoll's works. The phenomenon of such a building existing in a very small, unpretentious community was made all the more unbelievable after my first trip to Dowagiac. I quickly became an addict to the history of the Beckwith. The more I learned, the more I wanted to know. To properly appreciate the anachronism which the Beckwith represented, picture a one-industry village set in the midst of rolling farmlands. Run a major railroad through town with the west end anchored in Chicago and the eastern terminus in Detroit. While people today will jokingly declare, "The best thing out of Dowagiac is the train," seventy-five years ago no one would have considered such derision. Instead, the out-of-town visitor undoubtedly would have been asked, "Have you been in the Beckwith Theater yet? You must see it; it is magnificent."

After your tour, you probably would have asked, "Who, for heaven's sake is (or was) Philo D. Beckwith? Why did he ever put this gorgeous, palatial theater in Dowagiac?"

Philo D. Beckwith's career as a manufacturer began with an improved round seed drill, an agricultural implement. To launch his enterprise Beckwith had been forced to borrow capital, often at extravagant rates. On several occasions he had to pay twenty-five percent interest. He parlayed hard work, long hours, an iron will, and a good product into financial independence. At this point he turned his managerial skills to the mass production of a nineteenth century "necessity." The cast iron wood-burning stove and its counterpart, the cast iron wood-burning furnace, were both very much in demand. Within a short time, Beckwith's Round Oak Stove Company had established itself and orders came from near and far. Round Oak grew and rewarded Beckwith beyond anything he had envisioned when saddled with loans at twenty-five percent interest. As Round Oak prospered, so did Dowagiac. Round Oak was Dowagiac and Dowagiac was Beckwith.

Unlike many of the more well-known philanthropic entrepreneurs of the Gilded Age, P. D. Beckwith decided to bring culture to his home town rather than underwrite it in a big city. He truly believed in the civilizing and ennobling influence that a theater for the performing arts would have on the people of Dowagiac. He also wanted to make the townsfolk aware and appreciative of his personal pantheon of heroes and heroines whom he considered to be the true benefactors of the human race. The theater, therefore, would serve as a kind of art gallery, with sculptures and paintings, fine glass work, and grand appointments throughout.

Beckwith lived at a time when freethinkers and free thought enjoyed an unparalleled popularity in our country. At the head of the free-spirited rationalism was the incomparable orator, lecturer, lawyer, and Republican publicist, Colonel Robert Green Ingersoll. Ingersoll delighted SRO audiences in theaters, opera houses, and town halls for a quarter of a century, from New York to San Francisco, from Vancouver to Boston. The last twelve years of his life, 1887-1899, he lived in a town house in Grammercy Park, New York City. For weeks at a time he would leave his hearth and home and crisscross the country, delivering his iconoclastic attacks upon the excesses and cruelties of orthodox religion. He also lectured on Paine, Shakespeare, Burns, Lincoln, Voltaire, and many other notables. Beckwith admired Ingersoll intensely. Most everything Ingersoll endorsed in the arts and free thought, Beckwith adopted as a love of his own. In the period between the Civil War's end and the start of World War I, there was a grand optimism in our land. It was characterized by reform, reason, and creative free thought. Between 1865 and 1914, it was widely believed that, with a little more public education and the continuing advance of science and technology welded to America's industrial genius, the millennium would surely soon be here. No other apostle of reason and champion of confidence in the possibility of free people building a just and good society spoke to this point more vigorously than did Robert Ingersoll. His flights of oratory had no equal. Beckwith was one of the thousands who had heard and admired Ingersoll. He listened, spellbound, and then patterned his own credo on Ingersoll's "religion of humanity," a philosophy of loving living for the here and now.

Unfortunately, Beckwith did not live to fulfill his ambition of a grand theater for his hometown. He died suddenly in 1889. His heirs felt his loss acutely. What could be a more fitting memorial to him than a fine theater, such as Philo had envisioned? His heirs set to work at once. Money would be no object. The Beckwith legacy was very substantial; besides, this was a memorial to a grand humanitarian and lover of the arts. It was decided that the theater should be incorporated into a larger building which could house the home offices of the Round Oak Company. Its construction must have caused quite a stir in the Dowagiac of 1892. I wondered how the newspapers covered the building's construction and the week of dedicatory events. The microfilmed records of Dowagiac's newspapers revealed an unfortunate eight-year gap, 1892-1900. The local librarian was most apologetic but helpless. Even the Michigan State Historical Library did not have the missing years. Poking around in the back room of the present-day Dowagiac Daily News building, I found an unmarked, unlocked cabinet. Inside, dusty, and in no particular order, were the bound volumes for the missing years! One volume in particular caught my eye. On the binding in cracked gold lettering it declared, "1893." Gingerly I turned the fragile, yellowed pages of the Dowagiac *Republican*. There was the story, front page news for January 18, 1893. The article was several columns deep, its heading proudly declaring:

The Beckwith Memorial Theater Building
The finest theater in America

Dowagiac was justly proud of this beautiful building, erected as a tribute to the memory of one who did so much for its prosperity, P. D. Beckwith. After long introductory passages concerning the forthcoming opening night's performance of Shakespeare's *Much Ado,* starring Madame Rhea (with William S. Hart playing Dominick), followed by a tribute to the late

Philo D. Beckwith, the paper gets down to a detailed accounting of the handsome building itself. Let me share with you, verbatim, the article as it appeared to those who, in 1893, made it their daily habit to read the Dowagiac *Republican*:

> And so it has come to pass that this beautiful building is offered by the Beckwith estate as a tribute to his memory. A splendid act worthy of all commendation. Mr. Fred E. Lee, Mrs. Kate B. Lee, his wife, who is the daughter of Mr. Beckwith, her mother, Mrs. C. M. Beckwith, and A. B. Gardner, a grandson, are the ones to whom the credit of this beautiful act is due. The architect to whom the credit of designing is due is W. E. Brown, of Chicago.* In architectural treatment the building has the sturdy, noble outline of the Romanesque, embellished with the more refined detail of the Renaissance. The aim was to give it a true monumental effect and at the same time, to make it in a most convenient form for the practical uses to which it is to be devoted. How well that aim has been attained is proven by one look at the splendid front. The first story is an arcade of four great stone arches with rock-faced piers between. These arches each embrace a division of the building, leaving the entrance to the theater, the banking room, which will be occupied by Lee Bros. & Co.'s bank, and two stores, free from all obstruction. The arches show the whole depth of the wall and are carved on the edges and finished on the backs. The faces of the deep voussoirs are rock faced and have heavy label mouldings. The spandrils richly carved. The piers run up to the top of the wall as broad, shallow pilasters, strongly marking the main divisions of the building. Over the arches is a cornice with carved frieze, the line being carried across the pilasters, by a series of portrait heads of famous women, in high relief, forming a marked feature of the design. The relief portraits are of George Eliot, George Sand, Mary Anderson, Sara Bernhardt, Rachel, Foster Avery and Susan B. Anthony. Above this stage the stone is chiselled smooth, each bay having two wide windows; those of the second story having segment arched heads and carved in posts. A carved band divides the second and third stories. It is above this that the design is peculiar, and wherein the memorial character of the building is most strongly marked. The windows of the third story have semi-circular arches, with moulded labels and carved imposts and bosses. This forms a grand arcade across the front. Above this in the bay over the main entrance is

---

*Brown, I learned, was from Duluth, Minnesota.

a richly carved panel bearing the name Beckwith, and above this is a large portrait medallion of the late P. D. Beckwith, in whose memory the building is erected. In each of the remaining bays of the front are four portrait medallions, with two in the north bay. The two in the north bay are Beethoven and Chopin. In the front bays, those at the right of Mr. Beckwith, are Rossini, Wagner, Verdi and Liszt; and on his left are Voltaire, Ingersoll, Thomas Paine, Victor Hugo, R. W. Emerson, Walt Whitman, Shakespeare, and Goethe, being representatives of music, the drama, poetry, and philosophy, giving emphasis to the views of the late Mr. Beckwith. These are finely executed and authentic. Above the medallions is an embattled parapet with carved cherubs between the embrasures. The pilasters terminate with carved heads. This work is in stone throughout, and designed and executed in a highly artistic manner, intended to strongly mark the purpose and character of the building.

A grand recess porch leads from the street to the main hall. The screen between the porch and hall is a rich piece of woodwork in quarter sawed oak. The panels in this and the bank, and store windows looking out into the porch, are filled with high class art glass, which will have an extremely fine effect when lighted up at night.

The hall, eighteen feet wide, forms the entrance to the theater, also to Lee Bros. & Co.'s bank, and contains the main staircase to the offices above. It has also an entrance to one store. It has a rich finish to the doors, a panelled wainscot running up to and around the hall above, and a fine staircase all in finely worked quarter sawed oak. The floor is fine French mosaic. The bank has an exceedingly rich finish and fixtures of mahogany, Numidean marble, Japanese copper and art glass with French mosaic floor. Hall, bank, and stores are richly decorated in color.

The second floor has the council chamber and city marshal's office, main toilet rooms, and the offices of the Round Oak stove works. The third floor has a large, airy hall and elegant club rooms which are rented to the Modern Woodmen of America, for lodge rooms. The entire clear glass of the two fronts is the best polished plate.

At the rear of the main hall in the ground floor, is the entrance to the memorial theater. The entrance doors lead to a vestibule, beyond which is the main lobby, giving access to the foyer and containing the staircase to the balcony. The foyer is separated from the parquette by an open colonade which leaves a clear view of the entire ground floor. Until within very recent years a true conception of what a theater should be did not make itself manifest. Architects seemed too busy with beauty

lines and fine arrangements of auditoriums to give a thought to
that to which the whole theater was devoted, the stage. It is the
fitting and arrangement of the stage in the Beckwith Memorial
Theater, that the greatest care has been exercised to obtain the
best possible results, and a great degree of success has been obtained. To go into technicalities and the use of stage terms
would not be perhaps intelligible to our readers generally, so we
note only the main points. The stage is fifty by thirty-eight feet.
Up to the gridiron, from which is suspended by an elaborate system of lines and pulleys all of the stage settings it is possible to
use in the form of drop-curtains, is fifty feet, allowing ample
room for hoisting out of sight a whole screen in a few seconds,
and allowing rapid changing of scenes so necessary to the continuing of the action of a play and effects are made possible that
were unknown in the old days of sliding flats. To those acquainted with and interested in things theatrical and matters
pertaining to proper stage fitting we think it is a sufficient guarantee of the success of the stage to say that Albert, Grover &
Burridge, of Chicago, had the direction of the stage fittings and
the wall decorations of the auditorium and entire building.
Ernest Albert, of A., G., & B., under whose direction the art
glass, colorings, the selection of draperies, and furnishings of the
theater were made, has succeeded admirably in producing a
most beautiful and harmonious whole. The wall decorations are
executed in that daintiest and most refined of all styles of ornament, the First Empire, to harmonize with the architectural effects. The coloring of the lower walls is a soft beautiful tone into
which there enters the elements of red, a tinge of yellow and a
tone of gray. A color soft, warm and atmospheric, difficult to
describe but on which the beautiful empire ornaments are rendered in gold making a refined and lovely effect. From this
beautiful color it blends on the side walls in soft gradations up
into an apple green, making a scheme of color in all, that is like
the afterglow in a summer evening sky. The beautiful blending
of the shades of color, the gorgeous draperies and the elegant
plush covered opera chairs and carpets, under the glow of the
many hundred different colored electric lights, carries one to
dreamland. All of the designs used in the decoration are the
original designs of J. Frederic Scott, of the firm of Albert, Grover & Burridge. The drop-curtain was painted by another of the
firm, Oliver Dennet Grover, and is a dream of loveliness. It is
monumental in character, with male and female figures and
cupids representing the different elements of the drama, in a
Grecian landscape, where splendid temples set amid the cypress
and acacia backed up by faint lines of distant hills from the
background. The foreground is composed of terraces of marble

exquisitely rendered, on which recline the figures amid bloom-
ing flowers. Leaving the auditorium we emerge into the main entrance. Facing us is the great stone arch of the outer entrance
and we are not surprised at the transition from dainty empire
ornament to the strong oriental effect of the Romanesque.

The bank of Lee Bros. adjoining is in a way typical of
treasure, it being a rich effect of lacquers and transparent
colors, through which the gold and silver background peeps.
Quiet and refined in treatment, there is a feeling of richness and
solidity so much in harmony with the character of the place, a
treasure house. One of the most striking and beautiful features
of the whole building is the art glass used in the theater, in the
screen in the main hall and in the bank. It is here that the best
knowledge and artistic ability has been used in glass decoration.
To people who have used the word "stained glass", this will be a
revelation of beauty.

As remarkable as this detailed accounting is, perhaps even
more surprising is the generous treatment accorded Ingersoll
(often called "The Great Infidel" by the closed minds of his
day):

On the twenty-fifth of January, Col. Robert G. Ingersoll
will formally dedicate the theater and deliver an address on
Shakespeare. Who, at this day, is more worthy to speak of the
Bard of Avon, the myriad minded man, the greatest and most
human of all poets that ever lived, than our Robert G. Ingersoll,
whose matchless oratory has ever been lifted up and wrung into
the hearts and minds of man, with love for better nobler things.
No word that we can say, can add lustre to the fame of Ingersoll.
That we will love and understand the Bard of Avon better, or
that he will be worthy of his theme there can be no doubt. How
fitting, at such a time, amid the noble thoughts, the higher aspirations, the kindlier feelings for our fellowman, will come to
the memory of the man, Philo D. Beckwith, who lived and
labored here, and worked out his life plans among us; and to
whom this splendid temple of art has been dedicated as a
memorial.

Ingersoll's fame as an orator and iconoclast had made him
the most loved and hated man of his day. Taking stock of what
Darwin and T. H. Huxley had done to undermine the superstition and ignorance of the Bible's authors, Ingersoll built a
career around liberating the minds of the timid and fearful by

exposing the errors and absurdities of orthodoxy. He spoke with sarcasm, wit, and sincere hostility against the unmitigated horrors and cruelties of "hell and eternal damnation." He outdrew all other orators, clerical or otherwise. He simply had no competition.

In 1893, Dowagiac was not considered to be a hotbed of free thought. Nevertheless, Ingersoll's reception was generous, both in the press and at the Beckwith. In 1893, free thought was acceptable news and when it was embodied in the handsome presence and gorgeous rhetoric of "Royal Bob Ingersoll" it became front page copy. Consider these words which appeared in Dowagiac's second newspaper, *The Dowagiac Times*, for January 19, 1893, just six days before Ingersoll would deliver his dedicatory address at the Beckwith:

> That on the evening of January 25th we shall be able to sit in the finest equipped and decorated theater in America and listen to the greatest reasoner, advocate, poet and orator the world has ever known and all at home, seems more like a dream than a reality . . . Few of us agree with him in politics, religion, and all minor points but every good man and woman agrees in the supreme right to disagree. We would not wish to live in a world where honest discussion was a lost art . . . Ingersoll is not only the greatest living orator but incomparable in eloquence, poetry, logic, wit and general perspicuity of expression.

"We would not want to live in a world where honest discussion was a lost art." Between 1964-1974, the troubled decade dominated by Vietnam and Watergate, to what extent were we governed by this freethought sentiment of 1893? Let history answer that question.

Today, there is much talk about achieving the long-overdue equality of opportunity for women. What happened to the example set by the heirs of P. D. Beckwith in assigning the six most prominent positions of display on the theater's exterior to sculptures of six women, six creative free spirits? Was Beckwith (or his heirs) that far ahead of the times or was this merely indicative of the attitudes of the day? In the last quarter of the nineteenth century, women had many champions in their quest for suffrage and equal opportunity from within the ranks of free thinkers. In fact, many of the suffragists were free thinkers too:

Carrie Chapman Catt, Elizabeth Cady Stanton, and Ernestine Rose are three of them. It was no accident that women were given the place of prominence in the theater for all to see. Two full floors above the women, on the building's extensive facade, were depictions of fourteen famous men, each portrayed in a massive stone medallion, carefully set in the building's front wall. Each of these "giants," carved in red sandstone, had broken with convention and endowed humanity with immortal contributions. It was, indeed, a splendid pantheon that looked down on Dowagiac's main street. The fact that Ingersoll was included is not remarkable. Knowing Beckwith and the period, what would have been remarkable would have been his absence.

The Beckwith Theater functioned as a legitimate stage through the era of vaudeville and then was converted into a movie house in the 1920s. The movie theater died in the forties, succumbing to new buildings built especially for films. The stage became a restaurant. The once-plush seating was ripped out, the floor levelled and a pool hall built.

Shortly after World War II, the huge Beckwith medallion plummeted to the pavement, three floors below. Neglect invited vandalism. Decay, deterioration, and outright abuse forced the once grand memorial to Dowagiac's first citizen to be abandoned. In the 1950s, the owner offered it to the city fathers for a mere forty-five thousand dollars. (Some thought it could be made into a library and museum.) But it was turned down. In 1966, state building inspectors demanded that certain "repairs be made at once" or the building would have to be razed. Shortly thereafter, a Dowagiac businessman and retired Navy veteran, Bob Wilson, mailed a typed bona fide offer of fifty thousand dollars to purchase the crumbling building. He and several others saw the possibility of restoration for commercial purposes. Three days after he posted his offer, a permit was issued for the demolition of the Beckwith building.

It was not just the old-timers who wept at the demolition. A college student, David Bainbridge, agonized over the Beckwith's impending doom. He pleaded with the wrecking contractor: "Please, take the stone medallions to the campus of Southwestern Michigan College. It's just outside of town!" The contractor agreed. A total of fifteen sculptures survived the building's demolition. Young Bainbridge had high hopes of marshalling sufficient support to provide a permanent home for the survivors-in-stone from the Beckwith pantheon of heroic individuals.

In 1976, the stone medallions still lie unprotected in an open field where the contractor dropped them off ten years ago. Perhaps the prevailing attitude of many townspeople toward the medallions was expressed to me by a businessman who, for thirty years, passed the Beckwith daily. The sculptures were visible from his store window. I asked him, "Do you remember who the people were that made up the stone gallery on the old Beckwith?" He paused a moment and then said, "No, I don't remember their names but I do remember this. They were all atheists." He smiled; I left.

The Elysian Fields of America's car culture, the parking lot, has yet to desecrate the eighty-five by one hundred fifteen foot parcel of land where the Beckwith stood, "built to last three hundred years." A vacant weed-filled lot is now the theater's headstone.

Lost forever and with but scant record is "the finest theater in America." It was a loving memorial to an honest man and an era we shall not see again. All that remains is the nostalgic ache for an era when, in absolutely splendid surroundings, "Curtain Time!" was the prelude to unforgettable evenings in a very small town in southwestern Michigan.

APPENDIX II

DRESDEN AND GRAMMERCY PARK

Dresden

In 1921, ten years after Ingersoll's statue had been dedicated in Peoria, Illinois, a ceremony was held in Dresden, New York, Ingersoll's birthplace. It probably was not very good judgment to make the plain frame house of his birth into a memorial. Dresden, nestled on the west bank of Seneca Lake, was not (and has not become) a tourist attraction. Dresden is not on a well-travelled road. (Dowagiac, at least, was located on *the* railroad between Chicago and Detroit.) But Dresden was, after all, the scene of Ingersoll's birth, August 11, 1833. The village, however, played no significant part in Ingersoll's coming of age. As an adult, he hardly could have had any childhood memories of Dresden, having left there at such an early age. Nevertheless, twenty-two years after he died, dedicatory ceremonies were held at his birthplace. The weather was fair on August 11, 1921, though a shower threatened to ruin the day's festivities (already marred by an error on the lovely souvenir memorial booklet, the date of Ingersoll's death being incorrectly recorded as July *6th*, 1899). The rain, fortunately, was very light and brief. The day turned out to be a total success. The most significant aspect of the Dresden dedication is to be found in the composition of the General Committee responsible for the event. Surely, it is a compliment of the highest order to Ingersoll to have many distinguished people, such creative individuals, memorializing his birthplace nearly a quarter of a century after his death. Among the notables serving on the General Committee were: Dan Beard, Luther Burbank, "Joe" Cannon, Carrie Chapman Catt, Thomas Edison, Helen Gardener, Adolph Lewisohn, Edwin Markham, Julia Marlowe, Edgar Lee Masters, Thomas Mott Osborne, and Lorado Taft. Others who have not survived in the history books of today were from the worlds of art, politics, science, business and reform. Each was a vital and significant individual of the period. Each had loved Ingersoll.

Probably because of the geographical location of Dresden, this birthplace never became the attraction that sponsors hoped it would become. In the height of the McCarthy era an attempt to revitalize the memorial was made by holding another dedication ceremony. The General Committee for the 1954 ceremony was headed by Joseph Lewis. This committee's membership, however, could make no claim to such notables as its predecessor listed in 1921. By the 1970s the house was in very bad repair. Not long after the last grandchild, Eva Ingersoll Brown Wakefield, died, the house was put up for sale. By 1975 the house was no longer a memorial.

The Grammercy Park Residence

The last ten years of his life, Ingersoll lived at 52 Grammercy Park in New York City. It was at this residence that he regularly received a returning hero's welcome from his beloved wife and two daughters. He hated to be away from them and his home in Grammercy Park. It was this residence, more than any other, that was to be associated with his most active years on the lecture circuit.

In 1925 the residence was demolished and a hotel, the Grammercy Park Hotel, was built on the site. Friends of Ingersoll approached the owners for permission to fasten a plaque on the new building. It was to read:

> On this site was the home of Robert Green Ingersoll.
> He knew no fear except the fear of doing wrong.

The response to this request was prompt and affirmative. November 9, 1925, the day of the official dedication arrived and with it Edgar Lee Masters, who had written a special poem for the memorial. He read it to the small crowd which had come to mark the site where once The Great Agnostic had lived.

As fate would have it, other local news of the day pushed the account of the Grammercy Park ceremony to page eight of the *New York Herald Tribune*. The big local story on November 9, 1925, was Bishop Manning's laying the cornerstone of the Cathedral of St. John the Divine; also appearing as noteworthy that day was an item stating: "A Blue Law drafted in Colonial times to be Tested in 1925." And on November 8th, the New York papers had reported that the presiding judge at the Scopes Trial was urging that the teaching of evolution be barred from the public schools of New York. Also on the 8th, Benjamin Gitlow lost another appeal and was returned to prison to finish his sentence. Gitlow, a free speech victim, had evoked some of Justice Holmes' greatest prose; but as was so often the case, Holmes' rhetoric was but a "dissenting opinion." All in all, it must have appeared to devotées of Ingersoll that the nation was in full retreat from the frontiers he had boldly explored. In addition to the little ceremony in Grammercy Park, there was, however, one other encouraging note. *The New York Times* reported: "A. Wakefield Slaten will preach on: "Humanism—the New Religion.' " But half a century later who would even recognize Slaten's name, let alone support the religion of which he spoke? The members of the General Committee for the Grammercy Park affair surely must have believed there would be millions. The General Committee was the Dresden Committee all over again but even larger. The same notables were involved with the addition of such luminaries as: Chauncey Depew, Zona Gale, Hamlin Garland, Joseph Lewis, David Saville Muzzey (who, along with Lewis, would participate in the rededication of the Dresden home in 1954), James Harvey Robinson, Oscar Straus, and one of the most courageous humanitarians of the twentieth century, Margaret Sanger.

The most lasting memorial to Ingersoll, however, is not at any particular location. It is in the hearts and minds of all those whose lives have been enriched, consciously or unconsciously, by his legacy. No one who is loved is ever forgotten. At the ceremonies in Peoria in 1911, at Dresden in 1921, and at Grammercy Park in 1925, the people could say, "We loved you living and we love you now." Those of us who never thrilled to his oratorial genius, who never saw him in the flesh, love him for the lasting light he brought, which dispelled the darkness of centuries of ignorance, superstition, and crippling fear. He is immortal as long as memory lives.

APPENDIX III

THREE NIGHTS
TO REMEMBER

There is no way of accurately estimating the number of people who heard Ingersoll during his thirty years as America's premier orator. More often than not there was a standing-room-only crowd wherever he appeared.

I have selected three nights to be remembered, three exceptional appearances. Each, in its own way, established a record. Perhaps the most unbelievable gathering of the entire nineteenth century took place *indoors*, October 20, 1876. It was a Republican rally to get out the vote for the presidential candidate, Rutherford B. Hayes. Hayes, however, would not be the drawing card; he would not be in attendance. The crowd would gather to hear Ingersoll, who had been catapulted into the national spotlight with his nominating speech for James Blaine in June of 1876. The "Plumed Knight" speech did not carry the day for Blaine but won for Ingersoll the admiration of the Republicans of the nation. Over the next twenty years he would take the podium again and again on behalf of the Republican standard-bearer. Between 1876 and 1896 Ingersoll would devote more time to the lecture platform, the stump, and assaulting religious superstition than he would spend in the courtroom. It has been estimated that, at a dollar a head, his public speaking brought him in excess of one hundred thousand dollars a year in each of the last ten years of his life. There were, of course, many political gatherings where there was no admission fee, and these crowds were the largest. One such rally took place in Chicago's Interstate Industrial Arts Exposition Building, on October 20, 1876. Built in 1873 to house the latest gadgets, home furnishings, and domestic products, the Exposition Building was of staggering proportions. It was just one hundred feet less in length than three football fields laid end to end. It stood along Michigan Avenue, where today the Art Institute stands, a structure, incidentally, which it could have swallowed. The Exposition Building was two hundred feet in width, and the height of its three domes was one hundred sixty feet or the equivalent of a seventeen story building. Made entirely of steel and glass, it was free of columns or pillars. It was designed by W. W. Boyington. (He also designed Chicago's historic Water Tower, which still stands.) By any standards the Exposition Building was a mammoth hall. For the night of October 20, 1876, it had to be.

The crowd started arriving before six though the activities were scheduled for eight o'clock PM. By a quarter to eight every available seat and standing area in the building was occupied. Daredevil youths climbed and sat on girders. Others peeked in from precarious perches by skylights in the domes. The *Chicago Tribune* said in its front page story (the only article on page one) that there was ". . . an immense crowd of at least fifty thousand in number." One would be hard-pressed today to think of a building (excluding domed stadiums) that could accommodate such numbers. And, we must remember that there was no such thing as a public address system. In 1876, Edison obtained a patent for his first phonograph, but the public address system would not come into existence until the twentieth century. How many of the fifty thousand in attendance that night actually heard the speaker? We can only guess. What remains incredible is that fifty thousand would bother to crowd in, knowing full well that their chances of really hearing anything were very slim. Such was entertainment in the days before radio and television. And such was the magnetism of the incomparable Ingersoll.

What he said that night was largely a partisan harangue on the merits of the Republican party and the unmitigated evils of the Democrats, headed by Samuel Tilden. The Republican candidate had not been Ingersoll's personal choice. Just four months previously he had nominated James Blaine, but in a losing cause. In spite of Ingersoll's powerful oratory, the convention settled on Hayes, a dark-horse candidate. Characteristically, Ingersoll then threw his whole being into the campaign for his party's nominee. Ultimately, Hayes would be declared the winner in one of the most bitterly contested and controversial elections in our nation's history. A special election commission, voting strictly along party lines, would declare Hayes the President. The glorious response to Ingersoll's oratorical efforts that mild October night in Chicago hardly presaged the virtual deadlock recorded at the polls less than a month later.

The incredible crowd of October 20th was never duplicated. With the demolition of the Exposition Building just sixteen years later, there was no structure that could accommodate such numbers. Chicago, however, would again be the scene of another record-breaking crowd two decades later.

The presidential sweepstakes of 1896 pitted Republican McKinley against the Democrat, William Jennings Bryan, "the silver-tongued orator of the Platte River." Almost twenty years to the day, on October 8, 1896, Ingersoll appeared in Chicago again. This time, an enormous canvas tent had been erected at the intersection of Sacramento Avenue and Lake Street. Again, reporters from the *Chicago Tribune* were on the scene. They were enthused and wrote:

> Robert G. Ingersoll preached a sermon last night to almost twenty thousand people . . . three thousand more men and women stood outside of the great tent . . . and gladly caught the crumbs of oratory that fell outside the tent.

The enthusiastic response which Ingersoll received from his listerners that evening was customary. Only the number of people crowded into a tent was unusual. Newspaper reporters had long ago used up all of their superlatives; now there were only the numbers that varied in their accounts. Ingersoll was always the same: "spell-binding, witty, inspiring, logical, convincing, caustic, persuasive, delightful, sarcastic, magnificent, unsurpassed, unequalled, unique, gifted beyond words . . ." and on and on.

October 20, 1880
The Academy of Music
Brooklyn, New York

"The greatest political audience that
ever assembled in Brooklyn."

It was not just the crowd that was incredible, though not a foot of open space was anywhere to be found in the Academy that night. What made October 30, 1880, historic was that it brought together on the same platform Henry Ward Beecher, outstanding Congregationalist preacher, and Robert G. Ingersoll, incomparable agnostic. Beecher's introduction of Ingersoll went far beyond Christian charity; it reflected Beecher's genuine admiration for "the most brilliant speaker of the English tongue of all men on this globe." At the conclusion of his glowing introduction, Beecher exclaimed, "I consider it an honor to extend to him, as I do now, the warm, earnest, right hand of fellowship." The handshake was heard around the hall. The audience could not be contained. Shouts, applause, cheering, whistles, and clapping were deafening; for never before had a leading "divine" treated Ingersoll with such generosity and sincerity. Some wondered whether the Academy could survive the thunderous din as cheer after cheer rolled to the two smiling gentlemen on the stage.

What Ingersoll said on that night he had stated many times before during the campaign of 1880. This was his final appearance in Garfield's behalf and he made his usual strong partisan speech. It was very well received.

What would be remembered forever by those in attendance that night was Beecher and Ingersoll, together in the glow of great and sincere mutual admiration. Beecher would live just seven more years. When he died, Ingersoll gave an extended eulogy, concluding with:

> He was the greatest orator that stood within the pulpit's narrow curve . . . . There was no trace of bigot in his blood. He was a brave and generous man. With reverent hands, I place this tribute on his tomb.

There is every reason to believe that had Ingersoll preceded Beecher in death, Beecher would have done the same for him.

APPENDIX IV

ENCOMIUMS

There have been two major biographies of Ingersoll written since World War II. He has not been buried and forgotten. Nevertheless, it is astounding that most Americans today cannot identify Robert Ingersoll. Groping, individuals generally ask, "Didn't he have something to do with a pocket watch or the Ingersoll-Rand Corporation?" When you reply in the negative, the response is predictable and somewhat defensive: "Well, if he was so great, how come I never heard of him?" In the introductory biography of this book, I have endeavored to answer that question.

Another reason that you may not have heard of Ingersoll is that until this collection, there had not been a list of notables and their tributes to him. The encomiums included here do not represent all that was said about the man by his contemporaries. All negative comments, for example, have been omitted, their presence being one of the reasons for the relative obscurity of Ingersoll today. Thomas Paine suffered a similar fate. Had it not been for Ingersoll, Joseph Lewis, and a handful of others, it is doubtful that Paine would have gained entrance into the Hall of Fame of Great Americans in 1945.

Many of Paine's greatest critics also attacked Ingersoll. Often his severest detractors were "men-of-the-cloth," most of whom didn't draw in a lifetime the crowds that Ingersoll spoke to annually. The aroused clergymen who attacked him, however, are not remembered, except in the hearts of fundamentalist fanatics. The critics have earned no biographies.

What may surprise you in these encomiums are the many distinguished people who expressed admiration for Ingersoll. Unless you are an Ingersoll fan of long standing, the authors of these encomiums will be a distinct surprise to you. At best, religious nonconformity has always been suspect in America. Its devotées do not often declare in public. (Billy Graham's enormous popularity today is certainly not due to his being a religious noncomformist, let alone an infidel.)

It would have been impossible to include with the encomiums the expressions of regret and condolences that poured into the Ingersoll home following his sudden and peaceful death on July 21, 1899. In the week that followed, thousands of messages, cables, letters, poems, obituaries, and tributes from newspapers, clipped and pasted to plain paper, occupied the mind and heart of a grief-stricken but courageous Eva Ingersoll and her two daughters. Hundreds of letters, some written on expensive stationery but many on ruled notebook paper, were delivered day after day. Most of these hand-written condolences began with the same kind of introduction:

"Mrs. Ingersoll, you don't know me—we never met—but I just had to write to you and let you know how I mourn your dear husband's death. Several years ago he lectured in our city. The night I went, there wasn't an empty seat to be seen. For three hours he kept us spellbound. That night changed my life! I was freed at last from the terrors of my orthodox upbringing. Christianity was no longer to be feared. I will always be grateful to him . . . ."

It would take many volumes to reproduce all of these lovely tributes. Many notes were painstakingly lettered, the pages bound together with silk ribbons. Poems arrived, awkward little verses seeking to assuage the writer's pain by finding just the right combination of words and rhymes to somehow lessen the great loss. Words were not enough. As Ingersoll had often said, "I know how vain it is to gild a grief with words but I would take from death its every fear." The mourners held in common an appreciation for the magnitude of their loss.

Clara Barton—Founder of the American Red Cross

Writing from Mt. Vernon, Illinois, March 7, 1888, where she was responding to the needs of the recent, terrible flood, Clara Barton apologizes for suggesting that Robert Ingersoll might give a "benefit lecture for the flood's victims":

> . . . and you my friend, will forgive me, for your heart is so good and kind you can do no other way.
> With highest esteem and kindest remembrance to your wife and daughters, I am, Colonel,
>
> > Most Cordially Yours,
> > Clara Barton

Henry Ward Beecher—Clergyman

On the occasion of introducing Robert Green Ingersoll to another record-setting indoor crowd, this time in the Brooklyn Academy of Music, Henry Ward Beecher glowed:

> I now introduce to you . . . a man who—and I say this not flatteringly—is the most brilliant speaker of the English tongue of all men on this globe . . . under the lambent flow of his wit and magnificent antithesis we find the glorious flame of genius and honest thought.

D. M. Bennett—Editor/Publisher of "Truth Seeker"

> Every man who has a mind of his own, who enjoys the bold ut-
> terances of a brave exponent of Reason, Truth, and Mental Pro-
> gress, will hardly fail to have by him the inimitable orations of
> Robert G. Ingersoll.

T. A. Bland—Author/Historian

Writing in his "Pioneers of Progress," T. A. Bland states:

> He was a great orator, a wit, and humorist of a high order. He
> had a tender heart that was easily touched by the sorrows of
> others . . . since the days of Lincoln I have never known a man
> who could excel him as a story teller.

Paul Blouet (Max O'Rell)—French Satirist

> Mr. Ingersoll is not only America's greatest living orator, he is a
> great writer and a great thinker: an infusion, as it were, of John-
> son, Voltaire, and Milton.

William E. Borah—U.S. Senator

As a young man, Borah came across a copy of Ingersoll's famous "Mistakes of Moses." He was reading it with great interest
when his father came upon him. Father was very devout and did
not approve of Ingersoll, and the book was gone! Young Borah
noted:

> I went away disconsolate. I had no Ingersoll and the intellectual
> heavens were without a star.

Editor's Note: Borah did not agree with Ingersoll in nearly all theological questions.

Claude Bowers—Historian

While yet a young man, Bowers was attracted to Robert G. Ingersoll.

> Taking the study of orators seriously, I sought the advice of the

living masters. Robert G. Ingersoll had charmed me with his artistry and I had the audacity to appeal to him for advice.

George Brandes—Danish Literary Critic

In Ingersoll's mind common sense rose to genius.

Luther Burbank—Horticulturist

I do not think there is a person in this world who has been a more ardent admirer of him than I have been. His life and work have been an inspiration to the whole earth, shedding light in the dark places which so sadly needed light. His memory calls forth my most sincere homage, love, and esteem.

Editor's Note: Burbank requested that Ingersoll's tribute to his brother Ebon be read at Burbank's funeral service.

John Burroughs—Naturalist/Author

In his journal, Burroughs records:

On the night of 24th of April 1894, went up to hear and see Robert G. Ingersoll . . . His lecture was full of telling points, much sound argument and many eloquent passages.

He said to me that he was by no means so sure that immortality was desirable; he would name conditions before accepting it—unconditional immortality he would refuse.

Burroughs was also in attendance at Walt Whitman's funeral where Ingersoll delivered the eulogy. Later he wrote in his journal:

Ingersoll speaks—an eloquent and impressive oration. Shall always love him for it. Some passages in it will last.

Andrew Carnegie—Industrialist/Philanthropist

Upon receiving a handsome bound volume from Ingersoll, a book containing excerpts and gems from Ingersoll, Carnegie declared:

> . . . I am glad a selection of your pearls has been made—long
> have I quoted them. They are real, not imitation, and will give
> you a lasting place in the Republic of Letters.

And shortly after Ingersoll died, Carnegie wrote Eva:

> What a record—always right on every issue . . . One of the great
> characters of modern times and the greatest of orators.

Col. Clark E. Carr—Author/Lawyer/Public Servant

> He was the boldest . . . and most considerate man I ever knew.
> His was a nature that yielded to no obstacles, that could not be
> turned aside by the allurements of place or position . . . power
> . . . or favors of the opulent . . .
> Ingersoll has done more to reform the pulpit than any other
> man.

Carrie Chapman Catt—Suffragist

In her biography of Ms. Catt, Mary Grey Peck writes:

> In the eyes of the unprejudiced adolescent (Carrie) the elabor-
> ate theological commentary on the Bible went down like a pack
> of cards before Ingersoll's assault. Not only this, but she was
> seized with crusading fervor to spread the skeptic's ideas.

Editor's Note: See also Dresden and Grammercy Park dedication
ceremonies.

William E. Clark—Ex-clergyman/Freethinker

> The world is a better place to live in because Ingersoll lived in it.
> He helped to make living in *this* world popular . . . It was Inger-
> soll's inexhaustible fund of humor that enabled him to laugh the
> devil out of the pulpit . . . Humanity owes a debt of everlasting
> gratitude to this great and splendid man because he did so much
> toward rescuing the human mind from fear.

Caroline Bartlett Crane—Pastor, People's Church, Kalamazoo

It was the People's Church of Kalamazoo that Ingersoll visited and said that it was the "finest thing of its kind in the state if not the nation. If there were such a church in my home town and its members would permit me, I would join it."

A telegram dated July 22, 1899:

> My deepest sympathy is yours; he deserves immortality here and hereafter.

Shelby Cullom—U.S. Senator

> Robert G. Ingersoll was one of the most eloquent men whom I ever heard. He could utter the most beautiful sentiments in language equally beautiful.

Clarence Darrow—Lawyer

> I pay homage to Robert G. Ingersoll . . . His acts mark him as one of the bravest, grandest champions of human liberty the world has ever known.
>
> Ingersoll was a great man, a wonderful intellect, a great soul of matchless courage, one of the great men of the earth—and yet we have no right to bow down to his memory simply because he was great. Great orators, great soldiers, great lawyers, often use their gifts for a most unholy cause. We meet to pay a tribute of love and respect to him because he used his matchless power for the good of man.

Eugene Debs—Socialist Candidate for President

Of all of Ingersoll's admirers, Eugene Debs was one of the most enthusiastic and effusive. Some have found this admiration difficult to comprehend, for Debs and Ingersoll were at opposite ends of the political/economic spectrum! It was, however, Ingersoll's great humanitarianism and his sympathy for the plight of the working class that endeared him to the Socialist Debs who declared:

> He was the Shakespeare of oratory—the greatest the world has ever known. Ingersoll lived and died far in advance of his time . . . I loved him truly . . . The name of Ingersoll is revered in our house, worshipped by us all, and the date of his birth is holy in our calendar.

> I have never loved another mortal as I have loved Robert
> Green Ingersoll . . .

Five days after Ingersoll's death, Debs wrote to Mrs. Eva Ingersoll, saying, in part:

> We were inexpressibly shocked to hear of the sudden death of
> your dear husband and our best loved friend. Most tenderly do
> we sympathize with you, and all of yours in your great bereave-
> ment . . . Gifted with the rarest genius, in beautiful alliance with
> his heroism, his kindness and his boundless love, he made the
> name of Ingersoll immortal.
>
>   To me, he was an older brother and as I loved him living, so
> will I cherish his sweet memory forever.

Chauncey Depew—Orator/Republican Politician

> The outstanding feature of that convention (Rep. 1876) was the
> speech of Colonel Robert G. Ingersoll nominating Mr. Blaine.
> In its effect upon the audience, its reception by the country, and
> by itself as an effort of that kind it stands unprecedented and un-
> equalled . . . Not to have heard . . . Ingersoll was to have missed
> being for an evening under the spell of a magician.

Frederick Douglass—U.S. Minister to Haiti, Civil Rights Advo-
cate

In his biography of Ingersoll, Herman Kittredge indicates the
high esteem in which Douglass held Ingersoll, writing:

> Mr. Douglass is said to have stated that, of all the great men of
> his personal acquaintance, there had been only two in whose
> presence he could be without feeling that he was regarded as in-
> ferior to them—Abraham Lincoln and Robert Ingersoll.

On another occasion Douglass had the responsibility to introduce Robert G. Ingersoll as the principal speaker at a huge
gathering, largely black, assembled to protest the Supreme
Court's ruling which declared unconstitutional an omnibus civil
rights bill. Douglass simply recited Leigh Hunt's "Abou Ben
Adhem." That said all that needed to be said.

R. L. Duffus

On the occasion of the centenary of Ingersoll's birth, August 11, 1833, R. L. Duffus wrote an extended tribute which appeared in *The New York Times*. It was, perhaps, the only major recognition of the centenary in print!

> Ingersoll was a man who loved his fellows rather than one who hated God . . . One felt the tenderness of his heart in all he said and did—in his happy family life, in the magnitude and diversity of his friends, in the beautiful cadences of his voice . . . He believed what he was saying.

Thomas Alva Edison—Inventor/Industrialist

> Some day when the veil of superstition is lifted Ingersoll will stand out as a great man.
> I think that Ingersoll had all the attributes of a perfect man, and, in my opinion, no finer personality ever existed.

Edgar Fawcett—Author/Playwright

> So large is his charity, so rich his tenderness, that intimately to know him means an incessant stimulus. One can almost literally warm one's hand at him . . .

Fawcett also wrote an extended tribute in verse, which was read at a great memorial service in Chicago's Grand Opera House in October, 1901, two years after Ingersoll's death.

Henry M. Field—Clergyman

> Though Ingersoll was a captivating talker, he was far more than that: he was one of the finest orators the country ever produced . . . He was born to be an orator . . . to be frank, I must say that as Robert Ingersoll was unlike any other man I ever knew, I do not think I shall see his like again. Genius is subject to no law of succession or inheritance.

Editor's Note: The Ingersoll/Field debates were carried in the *North American Review* on many occasions. Field was not an agnostic.

W. C. Fields—Comedian

Ingersoll's love of the theater was deep and supportive. Many of his most intense admirers came from the world of theater.

> Why, if dogs had ever taken the pounding that's been handed out to John Barleycorn, dogs would have long ago sunk into the "tongueless silence of the dreamless dust" as good old Bob Ingersoll put it.

Minnie Madern Fiske—Actress

> In my humblest days in the theater, I was never in a place so lowly for Ingersoll to seek me out and I must have been one of many struggling beginners who found inspiration and cheer in the understanding of Robert Ingersoll . . .

Nathaniel French—Jurist

> I was impressed of course, by his unequalled eloquence but I was even more impressed by the sweetness of the disposition of the man than by the eloquence of the orator . . .

Ralph Henry Gabriel—Historian

> Ingersoll was a prophet of freedom . . . He defined the good in terms of men rather than of Gods.

Helen Gardener—Suffragist/Reformer/Government Worker

In 1921, Helen Gardener gave an extended tribute to Ingersoll. The occasion was the hanging of an oil portrait painting of him in the Myrtle Green Room in the Washington College of Law.

James Garfield

President Garfield, though worlds apart from Ingersoll in religion, stood in awe of the Great Agnostic's oratorical genius, saying:

> Ingersoll is a remarkable man of pictorial mind and wonderful command of language.

On another occasion, Garfield openly wept and embraced Ingersoll at the conclusion of an address he had just given before a crowd of thousands.

Hamlin Garland—Novelist

When Garland was a young man he attended a lecture on Shakespeare. The lecturer? Robert Green Ingersoll. Later he wrote of that memorable night:

> The stage was bare and he had no manuscript . . . I enjoyed the beauty of his phrasing and the almost unequalled magic of his voice. He was a master of colloquial speech. He eyed us and laughed at us and with us, challenged us, electrified us. At times his eloquence held us silent as images . . . His power over his auditors was absolute . . . For two hours, I listened rapt with interest and when I went away I had no regret for my dollar . . . I had heard Robert Ingersoll, our greatest orator.

Nat Goodwin—Actor

> I have hung on the words of brilliant Bob Ingersoll as they rolled from his colossal brain, gone from one table to another to find each one more attractive than the last.

C. T. Gorham—Biographer of Ingersoll

> Clearly Ingersoll was a man of genius . . . Intellect of a high order was in him united to moral excellence of a type which is comparatively rare in men.

Louise Guenther—Ingersoll's Housekeeper

> Mr. Ingersoll did not go to church but he was the best man on earth.

Ernest Haeckel—"The Darwin of Germany"

> Robert G. Ingersoll is the valorous champion in the struggle for truth.

E. Haldeman-Julius—Editor/Author/Publisher

Ingersoll loved the theater because he loved life . . . Ingersoll
was above all a lover of Shakespeare. His lecture on the Bard is
still in print and will be found in my list of larger books, where it
has an honored place among thirty Ingersollian works, all of
them important.

Joseph Hatton—British Author

Ingersoll is not like any talker I have known . . . Ingersoll has a
full and practical knowledge of the artifices of oratory. He was
never at a loss for a word . . . He is one of the most natural of
orators.

George Jacob Holyoake—British Agitator/Reformer

From England an aging and grief-stricken George Holyoake
cabled Eva Ingersoll:

It is as though a light had gone out of the world or a guiding star
had fallen from the firmament to learn of Colonel Ingersoll's
death.

Edgar "Ed" W. Howe—Newspaper Editor/Proprietor

Howe's memorial editorial, which appeared in the July 21, 1899,
edition of *The Atchison Daily-Globe*, was a journalistic triumph:

The death of Robert G. Ingersoll removed one of America's
greatest citizens. It is not popular to admire Ingersoll but his
brilliancy, his integrity and patriotism cannot be doubted. Had
not Ingersoll been frank enough to express his opinion on religion he would have been President of the United States. Hypocrisy in religion pays.
     There will come a time when public men may speak their
honest convictions in religion without being maligned by the ignorant and superstitious, but not yet.

Elbert Hubbard—Author/Editor/Publisher

This history of America's thought evolution can never be written and the name of Ingersoll left out. This man more than any other man of this century, made the clergy free. This earth is a better place and life and liberty are safer because Robert G. Ingersoll lived.

Personally, I lay no claim to being a better man nor a greater writer than Ingersoll.

Elbert Hubbard also records in his biography of Peter Cooper, a Unitarian who was most comfortable with Ingersoll's attacks upon orthodoxy, a historic occasion which brought the two together.

The reputation of Ingersoll had preceded him. He had given his lecture in Peoria, then in Chicago, and now he made bold to ask Peter Cooper for permission to use the historic hall. Cooper responded with eagerness. There was talk of a mob when the papers announced an "infidel speech".

The auspicious night came, and Peter Cooper introduced the speaker himself. He sat on the platform during the address at times applauding vigorously. It was an epoch but then Peter Cooper was an epoch-making man.

Edgar Dewitt Jones—Clergyman/Author

Of all the eloquent speakers America has produced, the most gorgeous rhetorician was Robert G. Ingersoll. He possessed all the qualities that are required for the perfect orator.

Herman Kittredge—Biographer of Ingersoll

In a letter to Eva Ingersoll shortly after her husband's death, Kittredge wrote:

The light of the century has gone out.

R. G. Knowles—Actor/Performer

No man in the world has been less understood and more maligned than Ingersoll. He was simple in his mode of living, and did more good than many noted philanthropists entirely without ostentation . . . Ingersoll might have been President of the United States had he but renounced his ideas concerning orthodox Christianity, but as he himself said, "If I am not true to myself how then could I be true to the people?"

Robert Marion LaFollette—U.S. Senator & Presidential Candidate (1924)

He was witty; he was droll; he was eloquent; he was as full of sentiment as an old violin . . . He was the greatest orator, I think, that I ever heard; and the greatest of his lectures . . . was the one on Shakespeare.

Ingersoll had a tremendous influence on me . . . he liberated my mind. Freedom was what he preached; he wanted the shackles off everywhere. He wanted me to think boldly about all things . . . He was a rare bold heroic figure.

Corliss Lamont—Author

In the United States the most effective single voice in the second half of the nineteenth century opposed to superstition was that of Robert G. Ingersoll. Ingersoll was one of the most alert thinkers and persuasive orators in the history of America.

Melville D. Landon—Humorist

Ingersoll is the John the Baptist of Agnosticism—an eloquent voice crying in the wilderness. In writing about eloquence and humor, you could no more leave out Ingersoll than the scientists could leave out Darwin, Huxley, and Herbert Spencer . . . We must love him for being the Apostle of Freedom.

Harold Laski—British Author/Economist/Political Scientist

Not indeed that the new Puritanism went unchallenged. Its historical foundations were ridiculed with sarcasm by the remarkable oratory of Robert G. Ingersoll, since Paine the most persuasive of American free-thinkers . . . he was everywhere influential.

Joseph Lewis—Author

Like Shakespeare, it is doubtful that there will ever live another man to possess Ingersoll's brilliance of language. His expressions glitter like diamonds and pearls. But it will not be many more years before the heart of humanity will be indelibly impressed with the genius of the Great Agnostic.

Joseph McCabe—Author/Former Catholic Priest

In his pamphlet tribute to Robert Green Ingersoll entitled "Benevolent Agnostic," McCabe refers to Ingersoll as:

> . . . the highest representative of Rationalist principles in the second half of the nineteenth century . . . Robert Ingersoll rendered mighty service above all others, by his oratory . . . There was a humanity in his actions which one rarely finds in the public conduct of men who publicly profess high ideals.

A. K. McClure—Editor/Author

> I never saw him ruffled in temper . . . No man ever lived a more blameless life personally than did Robert G. Ingersoll in both public and private . . . Even those who were his severest critics in life were compelled to pay the highest tribute to the intellectual power, to the purity of character and to the generous humanity of Robert G. Ingersoll.

Julia Marlowe—Actress

> The world has been strangely slow to recognize the life, mind, services and character of Robert G. Ingersoll . . . By this time we should be emancipated from these kindergarten processes and acknowledge that, whatever he may have thought about the Bible, there was no man of his times of a higher standard of personal morals and no home wherein the atmosphere spiritual and intellectual, was purer and nobler than his . . .
> He could recite whole plays from memory . . .

H. L. Mencken—Author/Critic

Writing some twenty-eight years after Ingersoll's death, the caustic Mencken observed:

> What this grand, gaudy unapproachable country needs and lacks is an Ingersoll . . . He drew immense crowds; he became eminent; he planted seeds of infidelity that still sprout in Harvard and Yale. Thousands abandoned their accustomed places of worship to listen to his appalling heresies, and great numbers of them never went back.

Michael Monahan—Author/Editor

> The circle of the man's philanthropy was complete. He filled the measure of patriotism, civic duty, of the sacred relations of husband and father, of generosity and kindness towards his fellowman. But he had committed treason against the Unknown and this, in spite of the fame and success which his talents commanded, made of him a social Pariah. The herd admired and envied his freedom, but for the most part, they gave him the road and went by on the other side.

James Parton—"Father of Modern Biography"

According to Parton's biographer, Milton E. Flower, Parton was:

> One who shared Ingersoll's views on philosophic questions and respected him for the good qualities which were lost on his detractors.

Alan Nevins—Historian

> It is perhaps not unfair to place the brilliant Robert G. Ingersoll among the iconoclasts, for while he was by no means without constructive ideas he took a keen delight in tearing down what he regarded as false gods, and exploding what he deemed dangerous superstitions . . . nearly all the freethinkers looked upon themselves as fighters for intellectual liberty and clear-eyed truth.

The Unveiling of the Statue in Peoria, Illinois, October 28, 1911

It was a lovely fall day and more than six thousand people were in attendance as the long-awaited statue was unveiled by Ingersoll's grandson, Robert Ingersoll Brown. There were, of course, many speeches that day and included in the memorial album were letters from Edison, Carnegie, Haeckel, and Andrew White (President of Cornell). Charles Francis Adams, great grandson of John Quincy Adams, declared:

> . . . instead of an enemy of religion Robert G. Ingersoll was one of its greatest champions and its truest friends . . .

The Honorable John J. Lentz said:

> There is but one Ingersoll in the history of the world and I am proud . . . to give my humble tribute to a man who helped to liberate you and me from the terrors of centuries of bigotry. Lincoln liberated the black man from physical bondage. Ingersoll liberated the white man from mental bondage. I would also honor Ingersoll for making one hundred thoughts grow in the minds of . . . men and women where no thoughts grew before.

A clergyman invited to participate in the ceremonies, the Rev. B. G. Carpenter, spoke briefly but to the point:

> I present Ingersoll to you, not only as the great emancipator but I present him to you as the prophet of the greatest religion the world will ever know—the prophet of the Religion of Humanity.

The festivities concluded, Mrs. Ingersoll and her two daughters mingled with the crowd and a lovely day was dying in the west when the last admirer left Glen Oak Park where the statue still stands today.

In 1933, on the one hundredth anniversary of Ingersoll's birth, the following editorial appeared in the *Peoria Journal*: *A Hundred Years Ago*

> A little group of Peorians do homage today to Robert Green Ingersoll, Peoria's most famous citizen, on this the centennial of his birth. Peoria has already honored Colonel Ingersoll by erecting a statue to him in Glen Oak park, where the memorial services will be held this evening.
>
> Many things have been said of Robert Ingersoll. He has been called atheist, infidel, the anti-Christ and Apostle of Unbelief. These descriptions are unfair. Ingersoll was a faithful man and one who believed deeply. His beliefs were not always orthodox, but they were sincere.
>
> Robert Ingersoll was born into a world desperately in need of him. Equipped with a keen analytical brain and a marvelous gift of oratory, he challenged smugness in the pulpit and in society. He broke down a dam of hypocrisy and contentment that was causing stagnation of brains, business, social and moral development. He inspired men to that most beautiful and painful of all human endeavors—thinking.

One cannot evaluate Ingersoll in a paragraph or a page. Indeed there is no need to do so. Ingersoll was a man called forth by the time in which he lived. He accomplished a necessary task and passed on. Like Darwin, Huxley and Spencer he has been criticized most savagely by those who never heard his voice or read his speeches. In essence he was an apostle of Liberty, in a land much in need of liberty.

Clarence Darrow says of Ingersoll: "It is a grand thing to go into the market place and defy the mob. It is heroic to go forth and speak the truth that is in you despite all that world. That is what Ingersoll did. The man who speaks all the truth that is in him, although all the world hisses him, is a sight of such moral grandeur that all mankind must bow down and honor him."

The specific work of Ingersoll was ephemeral. It was called forth by special occasion, and therefore is limited. Back of all his eloquence and energy, however, was a zeal for liberty and reverence for right. The world has not yet outgrown the need for this gospel.

Editor's Note: Several volumes would be needed to present all of the editorial comment that appeared the week after Ingersoll's death.

Channing Pollock—Novelist/Playwright/Lecturer

My outstanding hero was Colonel Robert G. Ingersoll, then considered a dangerous atheist though many of his skepticisms are now orthodox.

James Burton Pond—Lecture Manager

Colonel Robert G. Ingersoll was without a doubt one of the greatest popular orators of the age. . . . no nation can today produce his equal.

Charles Francis Potter—Clergyman/Author/Lecturer

Robert Ingersoll was the apostle of the religion of the unchurched. Had it not been for Ingersoll's anti-Christian views openly expressed, he could have been President of the United States.

Marilla M. Ricker—Attorney

Ingersoll was the truest American that America ever bore . . . He would take the case of a poor man into court without pay; he would give a young reporter an interview when he could sell every word for a dollar . . . Ingersoll was a great tender hearted man, full of kindness, full of good feeling, full of generous impulses. He was as sincere as a camera . . . No man ever loved the true, the good, and the beautiful in man, woman, and child more than he did. This was the holiest trinity to him . . . Ingersoll above all else was moved by the patient martyrdom of man. An hour of agony on the cross was nothing to the daily sufferings of the human race . . . He believed in humanity. In my opinion, no greater, grander, nobler man has ever passed through this world of ours than Robert G. Ingersoll.

James Whitcomb Riley—The Hoosier Poet

I love him, I respect him, I venerate his name, for the name of Robert Ingersoll and True Manhood are the same.

Edward Arlington Robinson—Poet

In his biography of Robinson, Herman Hagedorn writes:

Robinson approved of the bete noir of his generation, Robert Ingersoll, for exposing the absurdities of dogmatism.

Carl Sandburg—Poet

I would have walked miles to hear his rolling swinging words about Shakespeare or Burns.

Editor's Note: Sandburg had heard R.G.I. defending the gold standard and was unimpressed by the "content" but not by the peerless orator's skill.

Margaret Sanger—Founder of Birth Control Movement

Writing in her autobiography, Margaret Sanger recalls an incident when she was but ten years of age. Her father, a stone-cutter and monument/memorial maker, was a free spirit and devoted admirer of Ingersoll. He invited the Great Agnostic to come to Corning and deliver an address. Of her father's activities in behalf of controversial/radical causes, she wrote:

Father joined the Knights of Labor . . . and this did not endear

him to his clientele. Still less did his espousal of Colonel Robert
G. Ingersoll, a man after his own heart whose works he had
eagerly studied and used as texts. Sunday afternoon arrived and
father escorted "Colonel Bob" from the hotel to the hall. (The
hall was locked, intentionally, so the group adjourned to a nearby hill) . . . Those who came for discussion sat spellbound in a
ring around the standing orator.

Editor's Note: Though she could not recall what Ingersoll had said, the
impression was both positive and lasting. In 1925, thirty-two years
later, she gave her name to the General Committee dedicating a
plaque on the site of Ingersoll's Grammercy Park residence in New
York City.

Elizabeth Cady Stanton—Suffragist

I have heard the greatest orators of this century in England and
America . . . none of them ever equalled Robert Ingersoll in his
highest flights . . . I heard Mr. Ingersoll many years ago in Chicago. The hall seated five thousand people; every inch of standing room was occupied. This was the greatest triumph of oratory
I had ever witnessed.

And in a cable sent to Eva Ingersoll after learning of Ingersoll's
death:

No other death including my own family could have given me
such profound sorrow. No man of this century do I more rev-
erently worship.
The future historian will rank him as one of the heroes of the
nineteenth century.

Adlai Stevenson—Vice-President under Grover Cleveland

Rarely at any time or place have words been spoken more eloquent than fell from the lips of Lincoln and Ingersoll . . . . But
for his unbelief, whether political honors might have awaited
him cannot certainly be known.

Oscar S. Straus—Banker and Philanthropist

He abolished Hell and anchored Heaven on Earth! Robert Ingersoll had the eloquence of Webster and the genius for justice
and humanity of Lincoln. He had moral courage. He was a
modern Aristotle with the prophetic vision of an Isaiah.

J. T. Sunderland—Clergyman

A friend of Ingersoll for some fifteen years but with views essentially theistic, Sunderland, writing a decade after Ingersoll's death, assessed his importance to religion in these words:

> Perhaps the most important religious service of all that Mr. Ingersoll rendered to his generation was, that he startled it into thinking . . . Independent thinking is rare everywhere, but it is far more rare in connection with religion than anywhere else . . . In an age like ours, when brave and honest thinking is so much at a discount, and when such multitudes of men before they speak inquire, "What is politic? What is the popular thing to say?" We may well be grateful for the example of a man . . . who had the courage to think for himself and who dared to speak what he believed true. (1909)

Mary Church Terrell—Author/Lecturer

Writing in her autobiography, "A Colored Woman in a White World," Mary Church Terrell recalls an incident in which Ingersoll provided a very important opportunity to her brother who had graduated with high honors from law school but could not find a firm in which he could serve his apprenticeship and enter the New York bar. Someone suggested that he contact Robert Ingersoll.

> I once was invited to a luncheon in New York given by the widow of Colonel Robert G. Ingersoll, who was one of the best friends the colored people of this country ever had. I owe him a debt of personal gratitude because of what he rendered to my brother . . . my brother had the privilege, the advantage, and the honor of being admitted to the bar of New York from Robert Ingersoll's office . . . Brother said, "People were always running to Colonel Ingersoll for help. He was charitable and generous to everybody without regard to race, creed or color."

Editor's Note: "Brother Church" should have said "race, creed, color, or *sex*!" See Marilla Ricker.

Mark Twain—Author

Twain's admiration for Ingersoll bordered on idolatry:

I hear four speeches which I can never forget . . . one by that splendid old soul, Colonel Bob Ingersoll—Oh, it was just the supreme combination of words that was ever put together since the world began . . . Bob Ingersoll's music will sing through my memory always as the divinest that ever enchanted my ears.

Following Ingersoll's performance at a testimonial affair for U. S. Grant at the Palmer House in Chicago, Twain fired off these sentiments to friend William Dean Howells:

I doubt if America has seen anything quite equal to it. I am well satisfied I shall not see its equal again . . . I shall always see him, as he stood that night on a dinner-table under the flash of lights and banners in the midst of seven hundred frantic shouters, the most beautiful human creature that ever lived . . . You should have seen that vast house rise to its feet and you should have heard the hurricane that followed.

Of all men living and dead I love Ingersoll most! and lastly: Except for my daughter's, I have not grieved for any death as I have grieved for his.

Sidney Warren—Historian

The death of Ingersoll marked the passing of the last notable American freethinker. Others were to follow but none ever achieved the same degree of prominence . . . American agnosticism can hardly be discussed without the name of Ingersoll—indeed, the entire freethought movement was inseparably bound up with him.

Walt Whitman—Poet

The friendship between Walt Whitman and Ingersoll was deep and long. Whitman could pay no greater compliment to Ingersoll than to request his services for his funeral if he were to precede Ingersoll in death. He did.

Although Whitman possessed a strange and not entirely clear mysticism, he nevertheless admired Ingersoll intensely, saying:

Ingersoll is a man whose importance cannot be overfigured . . . his importance as a force, as consuming energy—a fiery blast for new virtues, which are only old virtues done over for honest use again.

and

Ingersoll is a prophet . . . Ingersoll stands for perfect poise, nonchalance, equability; he is nonconventional; runs on like a stream; is sweet, fluid—as they say in the Bible, like precious ointment.

Andrew Wylie—Jurist

Ingersoll was the greatest lawyer I ever met.

Mary Austin—novelist

In fact, one knows that in the light of history, he (RGI) must be reckoned as one of the notable liberators of American thought.

Joseph B. Foraker—(former) Governor of Ohio and (former) U. S. Senator

Finally, the day of the convention arrived. . . . The intellectual feature was the famous speech of RGI nominating James G. Blaine. From the first sentence until the last he (RGI) had the rapt attention of the convention, and all the great audience that filled the galleries. I have many times seen popular orators arouse great enthusiasm but I have never seen before or since anything equal to the effect of his eloquent and telling sentences.

J. A. Graves—author

I listened to such a verbal treat as I had never heard in my life. His (RGI's) presence was dignified, his voice resonant and sonorous, his diction perfect and his eloquence unsurpassed. No matter how much anyone might disagree with him, the sentiments he uttered, one had to give him due meed for his accomplishments as a most brilliant orator.

Carle Schurz—journalist/author/politician

In response to an inquiry regarding Ingersoll's Plumed Knight speech: "it was the most beautiful speech I ever heard!"

Oscar Wilde—playwright

On one of his many lecture tours in America, Wilde grew curious about this lecturer who could command a fee many times that paid to him. Later, after attending several of Ingersoll's lectures, Wilde said, "Robert Ingersoll is the most intelligent man in America."

Conspicuous by their absence in the foregoing list are many of the Republican luminaries of the late nineteenth century. Although they were often deeply indebted to Ingersoll for their good political fortune, they did not often admit their friendship in print. No man stumped harder for the party than did the indefatigable Ingersoll. No other person possessed his eloquence and his commitment to the politics of the GOP. Many of the politicians, applauding his political polemics, did not record in their memoirs or autobiographies even one word about the Great Agnostic.

Glory be to the people of the arts, the free spirits, and the thorough historians. We owe them a great debt for having had the courage to put in writing their true feelings about the beloved infidel of Grammercy Park, Washington, D.C., and Peoria, Illinois.

Epilogue

It is hard to believe that the Great Agnostic died, July 21, 1899. His insights, opinions, and commentaries frequently touch the very heart of a current problem, concern or prejudice. How unfortunate he is largely characterized as one who was merely "against the cherished traditions of his day." How unfair as well.

It is not hyperbole or inaccurate to state that Ingersoll was the outstanding spokesman for humanism, the religion of humanity, in the last century. That many of his hopes and visions have yet to be realized is hardly evidence of substantive weakness in his thought. The fault is in human weakness, timidity, and intellectual hypocrisy. In terms of human relations on this planet, there is little to criticize in the legacy of Robert Ingersoll. A lover of life, truth, reason and justice, always willing to extend to others every right he claimed for himself, he was indeed a humanitarian, a champion of the oppressed who avoided the dogmatism of "isms." Maybe through this little volume you will have obtained a new perspective on the living of your own life. If so, no greater memorial could be erected than this to this fearless crusader for a better life here and now.

Let me close with a favorite, saved until the very last. Few authors of any age could equal Ingersoll's ability to put whole oak trees into an acorn of thought. His abilities with the English language were equal to his courage to be himself and urge everyone else to do the same with loving conscience, reason and science as the holy trinity.

I think that I had better remain as I am. I had better follow the light of my reason, be true to myself, express my honest thoughts, and do the little I can for the destruction of superstition, the little I can for the development of the brain, for the increase of intellectual hospitality and the happiness of my fellow-beings. One world at a time.

APPENDIX V
ADDITIONS TO THE FIRST EDITION

The "Plumed Knight" Speech
Nominating James G. Blaine for President

Cincinnati, Ohio, June, 1876

Massachusetts may be satisfied with the loyalty of Benjamin H. Bristow; so am I; but if any man nominated by this convention cannot carry the State of Massachusetts, I am not satisfied with the loyalty of that State. If the nominee of this convention cannot carry the grand old Commonwealth of Massachusetts by seventy-five thousand majority, I would advise them to sell out Faneuil Hall as a Democratic headquarters. I would advise them to take from Bunker Hill that old monument of glory.

The Republicans of the United States demand as their leader in the great contest of 1876 a man of intelligence, a man of integrity, a man of well-known and approved political opinions. They demand a statesman; they demand a reformer after as well as before the election. They demand a politician in the highest, broadest and best sense—a man of superb moral courage. They demand a man acquainted with public affairs, with the wants of the people; with not only the requirements of the hour, but with the demands of the future.

They demand a man broad enough to comprehend the relations of this government to the other nations of the earth. They demand a man well versed in the powers, duties and prerogatives of each and every department of this government. They demand a man who will sacredly preserve the financial honor of the United States; one who knows enough to know that the national debt must be paid through the prosperity of this people; one who knows enough to know that all the financial theories in the world cannot redeem a single dollar; one who knows enough to know that all the money must be made, not by law, but by labor;

one who knows enough to know that the people of the United States have the industry to make the money, and the honor to pay it over just as fast as they make it.

The Republicans of the United States demand a man who knows that prosperity and resumption, when they come, must come together; that when they come, they will come hand in hand through the golden harvest fields; hand in hand by the whirling spindles and the turning wheels; hand in hand past the open furnace doors; hand in hand by the chimneys filled with eager fire, greeted and grasped by the countless sons of toil.

This money has to be dug out of the earth. You cannot make it by passing resolutions in a political convention.

The Republicans of the United States want a man who knows that this government should protect every citizen, at home and abroad; who knows that any government that will not defend its defenders, and protect its protectors, is a disgrace to the map of the world. They demand a man who believes in the eternal separation and divorcement of church and school. They demand a man whose political reputation is as spotless as a star; but they do not demand that their candidate shall have a certificate of moral character signed by a confederate congress. The man who has, in full, heaped and rounded measure, all these splendid qualifications, is the present grand and gallant leader of the Republican Party—James G. Blaine.

Our country, crowned with the vast and marvelous achievements of its first century, asks for a man worthy of the past, and prophetic of her future; asks for a man who has the audacity of genius; asks for a man who is the grandest combination of heart, conscience and brain beneath her flag—such a man is James G. Blaine.

For the Republican host, led by this intrepid man, there can be no defeat.

This is a grand year—a year filled with recollections of the Revolution; filled with the proud and tender memories of the past; with the sacred legends of liberty—a year in which the sons of freedom will drink from the fountains of enthusiasm; a year in which the people call for a man who has preserved in Congress what our soldiers won upon the field; a year in which they call for the man who has torn from the throat of treason the tongue of slander—for the man who has snatched the mask of Democracy from the hideous face of rebellion; for this man who, like an intellectual athlete, has stood in the arena of debate and challenged all comers, and who is still a total stranger to defeat.

Like an armed warrior, like a plumed knight, James G. Blaine marched down the halls of the American Congress and threw his shining lance full and fair against the brazen foreheads of the defamers of his country and the maligners of his honor. For the Republican Party to desert this gallant leader now, is as though an army should desert their general upon the field of battle.

James G. Blaine is now and has been for years the bearer of the sacred standard of the Republican Party. I call it sacred, because no human being can stand beneath its folds without becoming and without remaining free.

Gentlemen of the convention, in the name of our great Republic, the only Republic that ever existed upon this earth; in the name of all her defenders and of all her supporters; in the name of all her soldiers living; in the name of all her soldiers dead upon the field of battle, and in the name of those who perished in the skeleton clutch of famine at Andersonville and Libby, whose sufferings he so vividly remembers, Illinois—Illinois nominates for the next President of this country that prince of parliamentarians—that leader of leaders—James G. Blaine.